GOD IN AMERICA
Religion and Politics in the United States

FURIO COLOMBO

GOD IN AMERICA

Religion and Politics in the United States

TRANSLATED BY
Kristin Jarratt

COLUMBIA UNIVERSITY PRESS
NEW YORK   1984

Library of Congress Cataloging in Publication Data

Colombo, Furio.
  God in America.

  Translation of: Il Dio d'America.
  Includes index.
  1. United States—Religion—1960–   2. United
States—Politics and government—1981–   . I. Title.
BL2525.C6413 1984   291.1′77′0973   84-4278
ISBN 0-231-05972-8 (alk. paper)

Columbia University Press
New York   Guildford, Surrey
Copyright © 1984 Furio Colombo
All rights reserved

Printed in the United States of America

Translation of *Il Dio d'America*
© 1983 Arnoldo Mondadori Editore S.p.A., Milano

Clothbound editions of Columbia University Press Books are Smyth-sewn
and printed on permanent and durable acid-free paper.

Book Design by Ken Venezio.

Contents

Preface

"The writer of fiction," Italian novelist Alberto Moravia once said, "is like an artisan. He conceives his piece, he finishes it, he makes sure it works and then everything is done. Never ask a fiction writer to speak of his book. Good or bad, it will speak for itself." This peace of mind is not granted to the author of nonfiction. The anxiety remains: have I said everything that could be said (within the limits of the work) on the subject? Then uncertainty sets in: was my focus concentrated properly on what really matters? Does my material support my assumptions? Is the basic idea, the original motivation for which the book was written, useful and valid? To give a proper answer one must consider the crucial point of Time.

This book, patiently translated and carefully reviewed by Columbia University Press, appears in the United States more than two years after the Italian edition. Of course I am deeply grateful for the thoughtful suggestions, which entailed some rewriting, and for the indispensable assistance I received from the editors in doing so. It gave me the opportunity to keep, even to strengthen, my "foreign" point of view on religion and politics in the United States while reassessing and balancing factors, events, personages, and historical sequences I had originally conceived from a distant perspective. Yet timing is a factor for a study that intends to deal with contemporary events and to chronicle them while they are happening. Are they still happening? Is the American edition of *God in America* appearing "in time"?

Reading in the July 9, 1984, issue of the *New Republic* an article by William Lee Miller, "The Seminarian Strain: Church and Statesmen in the Democratic Party," I was comforted by the opening paragraph: "A curious feature of the campaign for the Democratic Presidential nomination seems to have gone unremarked. The candidate for the nomination had been reduced at the end to one Baptist preacher, one son of a Methodist minister, and one graduate of the Yale Divinity School."

I agree, that feature was and *is* unnoticed, yet it stands at the center of the political stage. Also the words William Lee Miller used at the time of his writing (1984) are almost identical to a key paragraph at the very beginning of this book, conceived in 1980. The problem is not a transient one. At the time, my preoccupation was, of course, to broaden the picture in order to remind the reader that the other side, the Republican one, is second to none in religious militancy, with the President of the United States boldly sponsoring all the basic religious assumptions of America's Fundamentalism, from the issue of the prayer in the school to "creationism," from the problem of legalized abortion to the one of public funding for private religious education.

Thus, something written under the provocation of the 1980 presidential campaign ("born again" Jimmy Carter against "moral Majority" champion Ronald Reagan, with evangelical preacher John Anderson as the third competitor) can still be useful to interpret the 1984 presidential campaign as the *New Republic* essay proves so competently. Reflecting on the intricate relationship between religion and politics in today's America, I believe I am offering to the reader something similar to the map of the so-called "Blue highways," that lesser known and very relevant network of roads which crosses the country and connects every point no matter how small or apparently insignificant.

But works like *God in America* usually have a motivation

deeper than the immediate occasion for which they were written. I want to reveal my motivation in order to clarify the way the material was researched and the facts assembled. Writing about the United States while in Europe, and then teaching Italian contemporary cultural events in America, I came to notice that a huge gap exists between information and understanding. It is always difficult for me to get my students at Barnard College and Columbia University in the habit of thinking that ideology is the key, when discussing Italian factual matters, personalities, and even popular cultural events (movies, novels). To a Christian Democrat to a Communist, to a Socialist in Italy, ideology is part of the explanation and part of the reason of almost everything. Ideological polarization matters also in deciphering the not-always-clear messages of the media, the headlines of the different newspapers, the way leaders talk at a public rally or in an interview.

My assumption in *God in America* is that religion is to American culture, politics, and life, what ideology is to French, Italian, Spanish, and other European cultures, politics, and life—a key, a matrix, a way of explaining and organizing otherwise confusing events.

I hope this presentation is persuasive. I trust the evidence is strong, both in terms of what is happening today, and in the search for historical reasons. It is a thesis that, of course, offers itself to the risk of paradox or to the appearance of exaggeration. It is not the key to everything, but I believe it is one of the keys to understanding today's America. It is encouraging to hear from authoritative sources that these facts "usually go unremarked." The purpose of this book is to contribute some information, some light, and a theory about the impact of religion on American public, political life.

GOD IN AMERICA
Religion and Politics in the United States

ONE

The Christian Heart
of the New World

THE debate will not soon be over. Was it the "new Christians" who pushed Amercia from Carter to Reagan, from liberalism to conservatism, from tolerance to intransigence regarding social issues, defense, economy, and ideology? And who are the new Christians? Why do they appear to be the advance guard of a religious and political army whose faith outweighs its charity, whose cry for justice overrules its need to forgive, and whose absolute certainty in its own principles makes it unable to comprehend contrasting convictions and beliefs? Several startling facts demonstrate the importance of these questions.

In 1980, for the first time in the history of the United States, all three condidates for the presidency were, and declared themselves to be, ardent Christians. This should not be confused with the generic religious belief that leads to the political ritual of calling upon God. Jimmy Carter, a Baptist, is among those who call themselves "born again in Christ." Carter says his life was suddenly changed by an inner light that showed him how to live a new life as a "pure Christian." John Anderson had long been an evangelical preacher before he went to Congress, and he too considers himself born again. In summer 1980, the third candidate, Ronald Reagan, introduced himself to a Dallas convention audience of evangelical and fundamentalist ministers by making two solemn declarations. The first: it is not you who give me your endorsement, but I who give you mine. The second: I am sure I am a "creationist."

If these are sincere statements and not mere political expedients, then they are a clear indication of unprecedented religious militancy. In the jargon of American neo-Christianity, a "creationist" is someone who believes literally in the Bible's words, even if this means repudiating science. By offering approval and support to the fundamentalists, Reagan was espousing a position of true Gospel-based Christianity, for out of that Dallas convention came the call for an end to church-state separation, as well as a proposal requiring that all American legislation be reviewed in the light of moral standards derived from the group's own interpretation of the Bible. But even if Reagan's statements were only the result of political strategy at election time, the question still remains: why would the candidate for a traditionally secular party solicit support from such an audacious and controversial religious faction?

Only twenty years earlier, during the Kennedy-Nixon race, one of the two candidates had been forced to defend his Catholic origins by assuring the electorate that he would never allow American politics to be influenced in any way by his faith. In 1980, Reagan decided he had to take the opposite oath, one his opponents Carter and Anderson had already taken.

In the presidential elections of 1984, once again a religious overtone became apparent when President Reagan, in a brief statement announcing he was a candidate, mentioned "the need to bring God back into the schools" as one of the basic reasons which compelled him to run. He was referring to the programmatic intention of Christian fundamentalist groups to reinstate prayer in the public schools system, overruling the Supreme Court's decision, which called such prayer unconstitutionl. Under the leadership of President Reagan, the "prayer issue" became a major topic of debate in Congress, bitterly dividing both Republicans and Democrats, in the House and in the Senate.

The controversy was also fueled by a strong statement against legal abortion previously made by President Reagan in his 1984

State of the Union address. His position on the legal abortion issue was consistent with the one taken by the large Christian coalition, the "Pro-Life" movement, which included Catholics as well as fundamentalists and evangelicals.

Reinforcing the new "Christian" image projected by the 1980 elections, the 1984 campaign presented a president with a conservative Christian orientation, an opponent, Senator Gary Hart, who was raised in a strict evangelical school and was a divinity school student at Yale and another, the Reverend Jesse Jackson, a Baptist minister, who applied the fervor of a fundamentalist preacher to propose a radical social program. It was noted by the press that the Reverend Jackson made a point of starting every political meeting with a prayer. This practice was in line with the "prayer in the school" position, even though a huge gap divides the left-wing fundamentalism of Jackson from the right-wing fundamentalism of the so-called neo-Christian coalition supporting President Reagan and endorsed by him.

The religious issue is therefore once again, and even more so than in 1980, at the center of a political confrontation. If attention keeps centering on the neo-Christian Right, the reason is not just the obvious vitality and the aggressive strategy of this aggregation of different churches and groups united under the conservative flag. It is rather that the new relevance of religion as a political issue is precisely the point of the neo-Christians' original purpose, and therefore, already a victory in itself, even without taking into account the outcome of the 1980 and 1984 elections.

In this light, the 1980 and 1984 presidential campaigns can be in part interpreted as a clash between two versions of Christianity, the fundamentalist and the liberal view, but also between the "insurgency" of small cities' evangelical preaching versus big cities' mainstream religious denominations. Of course other factors influenced the presidential race, from economic problems to defense, from the specter of weakness to the cry for a strong leader. What is more, as is always in this age of television when two images challenge each other, it is logical to assume that the most photogentic will win. But it is certainly proper to ask the question: weren't religion and religious polarizations strong new factors in the last two presidential elections?

Two months after the 1980 election, the authoritative Jewish review *Commentary* published the results of a study carried out by two political scientists, Lipset and Raab, who demonstrated that neo-Christianity had been overestimated. According to the two scholars, statistics and various types of evaluation showed that the neo-Christian movements had indeed been waging an excellent campaign for the promotion of their own image, but that they had made a smaller impact than it appeared. ("The Elections and the Evangelicals" by Seymour Martin Lipset and Earl Raab in *Commentary*, March 1981. See also Norman Podhoretz, "The New American Majority," *Commentary*, January 1981.)

However, only a few weeks before the Lipset-Raab report was announced, the American Jewish Committee had organized another study group which had judged the fundamentalist position to be noteworthy and not at all harmless, at least from the non-Christian point of view (Milton Ellerin and Alisa H. Kesten, November 18, 1980).

Certainly, the slogan launched by the Reverend Jerry Falwell, founder and leader of the neo-Christian political wing, the so-called Moral Majority, went on to become the war cry of the winning party in the 1980 presidential campaign. "I don't see," Falwell had said, "how one can claim to be both a Christian and a liberal." It may well be that the new Christians do not hold the center of the political stage, as they claim. What is certain is their dedication to a conservative creed they are convinced is firmly rooted in Christian faith. Furthermore, this was the faith that was proclaimed with equal passion by the coalition that enabled Reagan to win and will probably sustain and consolidate that support in public opinion and in Congress.

For instance, the American political leaders who were eliminated in the 1980 campaign—Senators Church, Culver,

McGovern, and Bayh and Congressmen Brademas—were defeated not by their own opponents on home turf, but by a national Christian coalition which blasted them for their "crimes" of supporting abortion and failing in their "Christian duty" to safeguard the country's defense. Second, when the American right's foremost expert on funding and organization, Richard Viguerie, published his manifesto for the new conservatism, *The New Right: We are Ready to Lead*, he asked Jerry Falwell, leader of the Moral Majority, to write the preface. Yet another example: when A. Bartlett Giamatti, president of Yale University, spoke for the opening of the 1981–82 academic year (and later repeated his words in the book *On Public Interest*, published in December 1981), he appealed to the intellectuals of the country to take the matter into their own hands, adding that "a wave of new bigotry is threatening the institutions of America."

Moreover, any political observer today must acknowledge a growing tendency among American leaders to act as if they held an outstanding debt toward the conservative Christian constituency, particularly in domestic affairs. In January 1982, the Reagan administration tarnished its own image by ordering the Treasury Department to restore tax-exempt status to institutions, mainly schools, that practice segregation. Today, the only segregated schools in America are part of a fundamentalist network of "Christian schools" affiliated with groups that belong to the New Christian Right. Best known among these institutions is Bob Jones University, which forbids its white students even to share their free time or private lives with black students or other black people. Segregation is a commitment each student must undertake "in his conscience" upon enrolling, because the directors of Bob Jones University claim it is a Bible teaching. Because this "university" has no accreditation and is not recognized in the American academic world, it might be easy to regard it as a culturally irrelevant and socially isolated private institution. Indeed, this was true prior to formation of the alliance that brought the "new Christian" to the forefront of the political scene or at least to the attention of the President, whose emphatic denial of allegations that he was reviving conditions for racial segregation does of course seem credible. It is true that there have been no indications of racism in American federal government, nor has racist policy ever been typical of the Republican Party. Nevertheless, Washington does give the impression that it has a commitment, promise, or debt to respect. Giving tax-exempt status to institutions like Bob Jones University is tantamount to contributing to the New Christian Right, and at a high cost in terms of public image and moral standing. It is perfectly possible that the administration overlooked the implications of racism, but it does seem to have calculated the favor, which it may have felt it owed the coalition.

This does not mean that the new Christians of Jerry Falwell's Moral Majority and the New Christian Right, and the conservatism now pervading the United States should cause shock or panic. What must be acknowledged are the religious implications behind this political direction, which have created a circumstance that elsewhere would be defined as ideological. It is certainly unusual for an electoral campaign to be carried out as though it were a confrontation between faiths or different interpretations of faith, within a Christian constituency that seems to have infringed upon the secularity that had always been attributed to American institutions.

Is this a revival—the word itself is a cornerstone in the religious glossary of American fundamentalist Protestantism—or is it something new? And how is it transforming American life and culture?

The answers to these questions can be traced back to the way the religions of each immigrant wave took root and confronted each other in America, resulting in a clash of hegemonies that finally led to one great armistice. In this chapter the examination of these developments should give us insight into some crucial questions: Is this interfaith armistice in danger? Is the independent and secular position of America's institutions in peril? And if such a threat does exist, why does it seem to be due to an almost symbiotic relationship between the political right and an emerging brand of Christian populism?

The story begins with the establishment of New World Prot-estantism, the most typical features of which are change, sep-aration, and the birth of new churches, in ongoing response to social and political mutation.

FERVOR AND PROLIFERATION: TRANSPLANTING THE PROTESTANT CULTURE TO AMERICA

When it arrived in the New World with all its various denom-inations, Protestantism was at once in its most fervid and most fragile, purest and most fractured state. The process of coloni-zation brought each of the European Protestant churches to the new continent. None disappeared, some weakened, each gen-erated new churches and cults, so that today Protestant Chris-tianity has the highest number of splinter groups known to any religion in the world. Certainly this process was helped by a condition of continuing migration, in which most newcomers to the territory pushed on almost at once toward the West, lured by an endless supply of space. Under these conditions, with its respect for individual responsibility, relatively easy access to leadership, and lay participation in church management, it was only natural that a robust Protestant culture would continually spawn fledgling groups.

New Americans all shared the same conflict. On the one hand, they needed to maintain and reaffirm the identity of their group but, conversely, it was just as important for them to adapt to surrounding conditions. This contradiction encouraged the growth of symbols, gestures, and rituals. At the same time it made it possible, even simple and tempting, to create new churches and cults. It is significant that today America is the only society in the world in which new cults, churches, sects, and religions can continue to propagate, and with such vitality that even the profound gap between Protestantism and Cathol-icism has been bridged, giving rise to the evangelical funda-mentalist movements. Older barrier have been surmounted, so that neo-Christian and neo Oriental cults have flourished among Catholic and Jewish children.

Another circumstance that has profoundly influenced the cultural and religious landscape of America is the limited or nonexistent interest in philosophy as a base of nonreligious knowledge and a description of reality. The absence of a coherent vision founded upon scientific thought or at least upon an outlook that stood apart and differed from religious faith could probably be attributed to the marginal relevance of authoritative intellectual groups during early stages of immigration that preceded this century. Rugged living conditions in the new settlements discouraged nonreligious introspection until much later. Indeed, some of the most prestigious institutions of higher learning started as schools of theology. For a long time, close ties between practical activity and religious belief left no room for an intellectual role, so that no European-type ideological polarizations could develop. At those times when American public opinion groups have felt compelled to support or repudiate such foreign revolutions as socialism and fascism, the motivation has always been based upon moral principle. Even in recent opposition to the Vietnam War, one could say that moral connotations outweighed the political ideological debate.

So it is not hard to understand the division and multiplication of faiths. The "culture of separation" has been a corollary to the necessary sense of practicality in life. At the same time, the homogeneous community, primary instrument of social order, has become increasingly revered. Although it lacked permanence and stability, the community tended to take the place of class structure, because it combined intense mobility and short-term rigid requirements for conformity. When a subgroup ceased to conform, it would break off, while an errant individual would face ostracism and, finally, expulsion. This all occurred within a framework of overall mobility that has given a transitory cast to American forms of bureaucracy and became as typical a feature as the basic adherence to religious values. While this pattern has not been clearly defined, it has been pervasive; rigorous conservation of the ritual has protected it. Each new splinter group has defended itself by creating new rites at once.

One example is the "revelation" that gave birth to the Mormon faith. Created *ex novo* one hundred and fifty years ago, today this ritual is conducted as an "ancient" cult, along the most severe and formal lines.

Thus Protestantism, with its infinite capacity for change and the generation of new sects, has become the cultural standard against which the other religious cultures have had to measure themselves, changing and adapting accordingly. Different ethnic groups have performed these changes in their own ways: Catholicism alone has been represented by the Irish, the Italians, the Polish, and several waves of Latin Americans.

In the first place, Protestantism was able naturally to ignite the New World with its own historical flame of "separatism" from stronger and older European institutions. Because of the very nature of its own beginnings, Protestant culture encourages changes and adaptations of its original models. As a result of the Protestant experience and historical vocation, the church could combine both components: rigorous belief in a few absolute principles, and flexibility toward economic, practical, and secular circumstances. Moreover, the American environment favored the infinite evolution of open religious forms, and thus another of the original goals of the Protestant movement was achieved. In this way, both the most reactionary fundamentalism and the most innovative experiences have found expression within the one vast field of Christian reference offered by Protestant culture.

So New World Protestantism has become the village banner, the frontier law, the rule of conduct for the newly formed community. Highly sensitive to the environment and the economy, it recognizes the need to create a new identification and set out new boundaries. For these reasons, it is also an excellent social and historical vehicle for intergroup division and antagonism and, in the end, for racism.

All of these groups share the same Bible, so that each subgroup has had to invest its identity in its leader, who might be likened to the founder of a club. Another typical feature of Prot-

estant culture, from the fundamentalists to the liberal reform-
ers, is a strong sense of belonging, as expressed in a few firmly
defined and staunchly respected values. It is the very absence
or scarcity of dogma that reinforces the historical rules of this
church-club. Because Protestant culture was born among national and regional groups that already possessed a strong sense
of identity and origin, and because each of these groups was
Eiropean and white, from the outset it seemed "natural" and
anything but inhuman to exclude blacks. After all, this was no
different from the exclusion of other church groups, particularly those groups that Protestant culture had fervently wished
to alienate or avoid. One such group were the Catholics. When
Protestant culture defines the space allotted to various religious
beliefs, the first criteria are whether they are foreign and how
alternative they are. The traditions of the South fostered the
strongest and "purest" form of Protestant culture, thanks to isolation from the church's original contacts and elaborations and
from the European intellectual ties that were never severed in
the Eastern seaboard states. In many areas of the South, Protestant culture defined itself most readily by exclusion: blacks,
Catholics, and Jews were all outsiders, and all were treated to
essentially the same type of "exclusion" for quite some time.

This is where the weakness and limits of American Protestant culture are to be found, inasmuch as racism and the need
to establish visible boundaries are signs of fear. And yet this
culture has proved to be so vigorous that it has deeply affected
not only the new American landscape, but also the behavior of
some of those it has excluded. It has forced Catholics, Jews,
and others to compete for affirmation, recognition, and success
according to rules that originated in Protestantism. These rules
still survive, with their strong accent on the individual and on
personal responsibility; on a sense of duty and its related sense
of guilt; and on respect for the truth, which is not subject to
the dogmatic interpretation of other religions, and so becomes
a practical personal commitment in daily life. These rules constitute a standard for every moral risk and every business ven-

ture, be they performed by one family or by the entire nation. There is no cynicism in this culture, rather the evident demand for clear-cut, stringent judgment. And this may explain why, for instance, modern Protestants favor the death penalty far more often than do Catholics or Jews.

If Protestant culture has found its place within industrial society (or is it the other way around?), it is thanks to corresponding needs: both have a variable set of values; both possess a strong sense of morality and a handful of simple and well-rooted certainties compatible with daily events, which must always be contained within a precise set of game rules. In this game, victory is proof of the truth; in other words, the winner has fulfilled a commitment undertaken between God and the good people. Clearly, this is far removed from Catholicism, where commitments take the form of dogma that operate on a one-way street skyward, where private behaviors and faults can be compensated with compassion, confession, and forgiveness, and faith must be completed by charity and social action.

Let us identify the three most visible features of Protestant culture. They are an inflexible God, a limitless horizon, and a gamebook of rules both fair and unfair. Fair, because they are established once and for all, with no cynicism, at the beginning of the game. Unfair, because birthright membership in the "club" plays a dramatically important part in the definition of personal destiny and thus affects one's chances of ever participating in the game.

The word "club" is used intentionally here to emphasize that Protestantism has never lost sight of the human, historical, and political circumstances surrounding its foundation, so that membership is more valued the farther back it goes. To belong is to be "noble." Not to belong is to be excluded from that nobility. Supposedly, God looks upon each of us in the same way. But the members of the club are asked to use a special eye for outsiders. Indeed, it is typical of American Protestant culture that its systems for regulating inclusion work beyond the confines of the church itself. As a result, religious exclusion may even produce secular discrimination or social snobbery, by assigning particular values to such distinctions as the one between Episcopalian and Unitarian. The overall strength of this value system has no match among the less "pure" Protestant cultures of Europe, nor does it exist, of course, among cultures dominated by one major religion.

Historically, this "inclusion-exclusion" system has been the most visible feature of American Protestantism and therefore of American culture. On the one hand, it is clearly manifested in the tendency to discriminate, while on the other it shows up in a propensity toward separation and formation of new clubs from the old generating, therefore, new opportunities to belong to a new club.

UTOPIA AND FUNDAMENTALISM: TWO WAYS TO VIEW THE WORLD

Given this much , what about tolerance, so often brandished as a historical value in America? How does it work? The only way to understand the whole picture is to examine two phenomena spawned and nourished to fundamental importance in America. The first is utopia which, in simplistic terms, might be called an overabundance of hope. The other side of the American Protestant coin is the need for absolute certainties, considered essential to the conquest of an unknown world. This requirement has generated fundamentalism, a fixed outlook on life that contrasts with the adventuresome thrust of utopia.

Utopia was one of the original raw materials used to build this country. It was soon strengthened by the inclusion-exclusion process, which some of the utopian movements accepted and others even helped to provoke. The utopism that found its way to America had three origins: one form had secular roots deriving from the cultural and social tensions about to explode in the French Revolution. Impetuous and agressive, heedless of obstacle, scornful of moderation, a second vision of utopia introduced America to the fervor of German romanticism; the

third brought a need for personal integrity directly transplanted from some of England's religious communities. These
three origins have always been visible in the various ways utopia has appeared and disappeared, only to be born again as an
integral part of American culture. At times the three have combined and at others they have divided, but utopia has always
played a paramount role in American life and social customs.

There are many good reasons to consider utopia an aspect of
religious sentiment. Some of the utopian communities have become churches, while others have joined existing denominations or caused splinter groups to leave one congregation and
form another. More often, utopian passion, its acts, and its
interpretation of reality have infiltrated all church and religious
organizations, noticeably affecting the Catholic and Jewish
communities as nowhere else in the world. Widespread movements such as the drive for peace and civil rights in the sixties
have possessed heavy religious overtones much more relevant
than political connotations. Furthermore, they have been fired
by a heady utopian fervor that has carried them to the very brink
of reality, or at least to the outer limits of the "reality" that has
been created by mass media and the common political interpretation of the facts. Both the "early utopia" found among religious and farming communities of the first settlements and the
"later utopia" of rebellion against the regulations of industrial
society have been more moral than political, more absolute than
democratic (in terms of democracy's rituals), and more religious
than ideological. What is more, both utopias have been powerful enough to produce political and organizational changes.

Utopia can be found throughout American religion. Its mighty
faith and boundless passion show up in drastically different political persuasions, alternating a search for the absolute with a
yearning for transformation. Utopia's immovable requirements
begin with each believer; its obligations are all-inclusive and
implacable. But in America the force of utopia has traditionally
swung toward reform, criticism, protest, and opposition. Its
continual migration toward forms of heresy that champion the

new and different, or toward denunciation and protest, can be explained in the natural, almost inherent alienation of utopian thought from stable and immutable institutions. The longing, the impetus, the search, and the hope are all absolute, but these are absolutes that will not tolerate imprisonment before any altar. Each of the many momentary victories gained in the history of American utopism has signaled a shift of hope, as the search for morality that fuels utopian fervor seeks new territories, causes, and confrontations. Utopia must occasionally wade through the marshlands of neglect and inertia, but the possibility for a sudden rebirth of passion never dies.

The other American tendency, fundamentalism, has been every bit as rigid and momentous as utopia. Like its counterpart, fundamentalism comes from a combination of religion-inspired rules, an elusive relationship with culture, an absolute need for truth, and intense faith. Its principles are even more unalterable than the Catholic creeds, because they are internalized instead of iterated in the form of cultural dictates. The movement's obsessive reaffirmation of these principles works in close collaboration with its strict rituality. This is the reason for the power and continuity of America's fundamentalist groups.

Like utopia, fundamentalism is not a church or a sect; it is an attitude that shows up throughout American religious belief. If Protestant churches are more vulnerable to it, this is due to the nature of their dogmatic structure, which is newer therefore more vulnerable than those of the Catholic Church and Jewish faith. But fundamentalist and utopian traits do appear in some aspects of the Catholic and Hebrew cultures, and this shows just how agile and forceful Protestantism has been in affecting religious institutions with much deeper and older historical roots than its own.

The fundamentalist attitude has left its strong mark on many religious groups and congregations and has firm and recognizable characteristics. Information is carefully controlled, while the sourcebooks of faith—the Scriptures—are greatly exalted. At the same time, every chance to adapt to other views is definitely denied. Some faiths, including Catholicism, possess a vast body of theological doctrine, whereas the Hebrew religion has filtered the Word through successive interpretative adjustments. The historical intransigence of the fundamentalist groups has inevitably been expressed on the one hand in rigorous affirmation of a few rigid principles, and on the other in the practice of excluding or condemning outsiders to the faith. Fundamentalism has served as an impenetrable armor to preserve segments and aspects of American organization and society. Its most dramatic guideline has been the separation between black and white.

Even fundamentalism has been known to venture onto new ground. For instance, it was certainly a fundamentalist seed that germinated the Church of Jesus Christ of Latter-day Saints, as the Mormons call their movement. Having bequeathed itself a heritage of written laws and thus become perhaps the only new Protestant church to succumb to the lure of Catholic dogma, the Mormon church immediately established exclusion of blacks, maintaining this rule until it came up against the whole array of American law and institutional force. But by that time, this church had acquired so much ecclesiastical might and prestige that it could afford to make practical adjustments that once would have been considered a violation of principles.

THE DREAM OF INSTANT SALVATION

The only way to fully comprehend the affinities and oppositions linking utopia and fundamentalism is to compare two other phenomena which have played a unique role in American Protestant tradition and world Christianity: the Baptist congregations and evangelicalism. Both movements originate in a passionate belief in regeneration, in the role of the holy mission, and in the chance not only to find salvation but to give it as well. Although the basic core of these beliefs is quite rigid, both movements are so anxious to extend their preaching that they have sometimes violated the rigor of the ritual and the rule of the absolute inherent in the fundamentalist persuasion. In so doing, they have amassed enormous religious followings capable of consolidating, separating, splintering, and reorganizing the Protestant faith by constantly changing location and time, as well as social, regional, and economic status.

Typically, the Baptist churches are founded upon a basic ecumenism; the congregation is typically an agrarian-suburban population that is linked to the land and removed, as a whole, from the urban culture of America. On the other hand, evangelism has been more lively and adventuresome, benefiting from its incorporation of America's original nomadism. The Baptist church and the evangelical movements share their faith that the nonbeliever can find spiritual regeneration, not by turning to such mechanisms as confession, but through authentic psycho-spiritual rebirth. This dramatic operation may range from the adult baptism of the "born again" to the passionate preachings of the faith healers. Thus the Baptist church has spread on a local and territorial basis, whereas evangelism has transformed itself into a migratory movement whose structure enables it to outperform other churches. Lately, its Christian revivalist crusades have even begun to erode the classic and intractable resistance of the Catholic Church.

The neo-Christian organizations have operated within the sphere of these large religious aggregations. Forming closed, secretive, conspiratory cults, they have taken American culture by surprise, and such sects as the Unification Church, the Jesus Children movement, and dozens of other neo-Christian groups have made an even greater impact than evangelicalism. As an example, for the first time in the history of Judeo-Christian relations, the new-Christian sects have been able to intercept part of the young Jewish population, setting a unique precedent. This fact is made evident by the frequent articles and editorials expressing alarm published in the last few years by the Jewish press in America (especially the *Jewish Week–American Examiner*) and by lectures and publications aimed at countering the neo-Christian pressure, such as Professor Trude

Weiss-Rosmarin's lectures or Shlomo Sherman's book, *Escape from Jesus* (1983).

It must never be forgotten that almost all the new territory covered by these Christian and neo-Christian movements is white. Certainly, it cannot be said that such discrimination has ever been based upon principle, whether here or in fundamentalist Protestantism, and it is certainly true that there have been areas in which the two ethnic groups have overlapped or interexchanged. But these juxtaposed areas are not typical, and when they do occur they are one-way passages, so that white evangelists may have black followers, but the opposite almost never is true. The Baptist churches have tended toward duplication and self-reproduction, with white Baptist churches and black Baptist churches that seldom combine. As recently as 1976, the pastor of the Baptist church in Plains, Georgia, were Jimmy Carter originally worshiped, was fired by his congregation for attempting to integrate his church.

It should also be borne in mind that almost all the neo-Christian movements that have proliferated since 1960 have been exclusively white, with the lone exception of the People's Temple, the suicide cult begun by Reverend Jim Jones. But even the new "secular" cults and the recent crop of parareligious organizations such as the est movement, which concentrate on the social and psychological reorganization of life, are all dedicated to whites. This phenomenon should be carefully considered, because these groups show no visible signs of the original "frontier-style" fundamentalism that is historically responsible for segregation inspired by theology or principle.

IS THERE A BLACK CHURCH IN AMERICA?

Within this social, cultural, and religious framework, the place held by black spirituality goes back to the early Christian conversion of the African slaves, with high points of religious intensity during the civil rights battles of the 1960s. It has had, most of the time, good if distant relations with the Catholic

Church. Similarly, black religion has easily established ties with American Jewish culture, at least during the hottest moments of the civil rights struggle, thanks to a comparable history of rejection or exclusion. Still, as we have seen, the black church's roots and, in the end, condition of separation and confrontation are truly shared with Protestant culture. The black churches form a splinter group in a culture founded by splinter groups; in this sense, they propagate and disperse without trauma, carrying the seeds of white Christianity to a cultural terrain rendered different by segregation. As a consequence, this religious faith is all the more intense, fervent, and separated.

When it crosses the line into black society, Protestant culture retains its endless flexibility, but it gives up the feature of exclusion inasmuch as it becomes the religion of an outcast society. As interest in immutable ritual abates, the same group or denomination can evolve more freely. Each church has greater autonomy, but this means there is less need to create splinter beliefs. The more intensely the ritual is practiced—with chants and physical participation, for instance—the less call there is for pure and stylized evocation. At the same time, the church becomes a civic and cultural center. This, too, is not a new role for Protestant churches. But among blacks this role is played with special feeling, because the church is the only interfamily and community institution that exists for a group which originally was neither a community nor a family.

Furthermore, the black church must shoulder the burdens not only of restraining the tensions, fears, anxieties, and uncertainties of the group but also of reconciling the different historical settings and variations of black Christianity. So the religious fervor is greater, but there is also room for initiative and personalization of the cult, something the white church has never known. In America, only black churches devote so much energy to the physical celebration of faith, while almost ignoring maintenance of the cult's formal rules. Thus the myth, in the form of church, community, and the object of faith, is far more important than the ritual. In these churches the skeletal dogmatics of the Protestant church have been adjusted to accommodate a boundless thirst for spirituality. But the most important change is the disappearance of the clublike organization, with its negative definition by exclusion.

As for the liturgy, when repetition and the respect for tradition fall off, there is more room for creativity in the way the ritual is adorned, colored, interpreted, chanted, and experienced. The love-justice relationship, which leans toward justice throughout almost all of Protestant Christianity, overwhelmingly shifts to love during the segregation phase. As a consequence, when the community is ready to generate demands upon society, it can invest them with values that are no longer formal or symbolic. Such typically black values as solidarity, charity, and compassion have played a far smaller role in the white Protestant church.

The feeling of exile and progress toward a promised land likens black religions to the original sense of Hebrew culture. The concern with brotherhood and love makes Catholic culture easy to understand, although these similarities are never stated formally. The ability to regroup continually into new communities, as well as the emphasis on organizational flexibility and civic commitment, have all been inherited from the Protestant faith. The intense and fervid faith shares common ground with evangelism. But black religion is historically and culturally unique; it is far more than just the sum or remnants of other faiths. In identifying the reasons for this singularity, we can define the black church.

The American black community was born in the midst of slavery, a deracination with no precedent or parallel in the history of recent centuries. Language, culture, memory, objects, habits, rites, and environment were all consigned to oblivion. Inevitably, one of the long-lasting effects of this trauma was a dream, indicating that suffering had been deeply internalized. This dream is awash with recollections of former myths and rituals. It never really dies, but it can never be reborn, either, so that Christian preachings have really only been grafted onto an imperfectly amputated limb. For a variety of reasons, the graft has taken hold. The most superficial of those reasons are the chance to learn, access to otherwise forbidden forms of expression, and the opportunity to create an organizational nucleus which may be "inferior" but still resembles that of the whites and makes it possible to participate in the community. The deeper reasons have to do with an obscure feeling not of revelation but of "rediscovery." It is interesting to note that among all the forms of rebellion and separation that have been used by the black community in its attempts to disengage from white society, the religious factor as a strong point of alternative identity has appeared in the Black Muslim movement. But that movement was mostly an urban phenomenon fired by mass communications, with their media blitz on the reawakening of the Third World and its "Muslim" and "nonwhite" revolutions. And the movement did indeed peter out quite rapidly. In any case, it in no way matched the mass participation in all the endless varieties of Christianity that constitute black religious belief in America. One reason for this—although the idea has not been thoroughly investigated by anthropological and sociological studies of America's black communities—might be that Christianity has represented an unconscious but no less tenacious rediscovery of the dream. The archetypal elements of death and resurrection, loss and recovery of the homeland, slavery and redemption, guilt and labor resound in the desperate search for bygone mysteries and beliefs whose loss triggered an unbearable feeling of emptiness.

Despite all the variations, the sweeping adjustments and the prolific formation of separate sects and rites, American black Christianity has remained substantially immune to the cults that have flourished among other African exiles, spawning such historical hybrids as the voodoo and magic found in the Caribbean and Latin America. In the United States, any signs of such cults are limited to the recent immigrants who imported them; furthermore, they have shown no tendency to spread. This poses an interesting problem: might it be that Catholicism, a culture within which para-Christian hybrids have been able to take root and propagate, is more susceptible than Protestantism to contamination by magic and "pagan" rituals?

The answer to this question harks back to history, culture, and the environment. Catholicism itself is a rigid and impermeable religious structure, but it possesses a highly visible "full" ritual, that is, a ritual full of symbolic acts, whereas a more typical character of the Protestant churches is a more sober and austere way of celebrating religious events.

It may be useful to dwell for a moment on the two terms "full" and "empty." Catholic ritual centers upon the tabernacle, or the "living presence of Christ," which offers the believer concrete evidence and represents an invitation to witness the physical reality of the Church, not only as an institution and a community of followers but also as a building that is literally "full of God." On the other hand, the Protestant ritual is usually based much more on community and personal relations—the pastor and his flock singing and praying. Holy objects and sacred materials are not enshrined in most Protestant churches. Therefore these churches may appear, to the eyes of a Catholic believer, more like meeting halls than consecrated structures.

When these two forms of culture and psychological perception of them are attacked by myths, particularly if these myths are invested with magic and evocative powers, history seems to indicate that the "full" structure of a church will attract the "full" ritual, that is, a ritual exuberant and rich. Those whose lives are already steeped in practice of a "full" cult can be induced to transfer their theological persuasions to symbolism. Thus they are open to magical beliefs that appear to be similar or complementary because of the familiar way in which they suggest that God is "present"; i.e., that they are "full of God."

It can be an interesting anthropological exercise to compare two New York taxis, one driven by a Haitian and the other by an American black. The Protestant's car usually shows no signs of his faith. The Catholic may be tempted to display a string of rosary beads, one sign of the "full" ritual. The cabbie who has recently arrived from West Indies or the Caribbean drives a taxi that is "full" of religion in the form of amulets and mysterious markings, not to mention brightly colored rosettes, tinfoil, and shiny objects. But the Protestant quality of austerity has always dominated American black culture. As intense as it is, religious feeling is represented by a few essential symbols, and these are more likely to be portraits of leaders like Martin Luther King or Malcolm X than sacred images or "magic" amulets.

The dwellings of Catholic immigrants from the Caribbean display a profusion of religious symbols indicative of the progressive transformation of faith into magic, a forceful attempt to fill the void. This may be a response to the obvious fear that the void will be empty and remain untouched by the physical signs of whatever faith the group wants to incarnate. In this sense it may be said that at the most elementary levels of religious practice, Protestant teachings in the "empty" churches of the North American black are better able to resist the irrational and the magic than Catholic churches in areas of intense recent immigration. Perhaps the intense proliferation of magic symbols is seen as similar to the nature of the tabernacle which is "full of God." Naturally, preaching founded upon the expectation and demonstration of miracles is equally intense among black Protestants and Catholics, so that the contrast proposed here refers more to style than content. In different ways, the desire for a miracle—the seemingly impossible transformation out of an actual situation that is too painful to be readily accepted—seems to be directly proportionate to the historical and economic conditions surrounding both these religious communities.

From the very beginning, black churches have assigned special importance to community service and to their role as civic centers, and these functions have grown steadily along with the institutions. For many decades the churches concentrated on consolation, support, and solidarity within the group, but later these activities evolved into a political attitude. Any explanation of these circumstances should take several points into account:

1. The worshipers come from a population whose only certain protection is provided by the church.
2. Group culture has derived almost exclusively from events and rituals celebrated at church. The restrictions which kept blacks out of schools and prevented them from sharing public life for so long created a natural need for the church to fill those gaps, and once this function took hold, it was never uprooted.
3. For most black people, the organizational roles generally performed by labor unions and political parties—i.e., awareness of group and community problems and an alternative evaluation of external "justice"—could only be carried out by the churches and their congregations.
4. Blacks could be leaders only in their churches. Later, it was natural for church leaders to expand their authority to include civil and legal activities, as well as defense and aid. As a black middle class began to take shape, the logical venue for its growth and affirmation was within the congregation, and only here could such leadership and hegemony flourish.

Black literature and the evolution of Negro music also prove this to be true. As James Baldwin said and Le Roi Jones repeated in *History of the Blues,* the black writing of the fifties and sixties was directly affected by the type of education received in church, in terms of language, imagination, and perception of the reality at large.

When the time came for the black community to mount the enormous political campaign that lay behind the civil rights struggle, the church was the natural setting and its ministers were the inevitable leaders. As we have already said, there have been sporadic instances of alternate leadership, with the Black Muslims on the religious front and such "neosocialist" groups as Black Power, the Black Panthers, the Soledad Brothers, and Angela Davis' orthodox Marxism on the political and ideological fronts. All these groups had disappeared within a few years. Some were gone after only a few months. But Martin Luther King's religious and civil rights movements led to many irrevocable social, legal, and political changes throughout America, and the black leaders of the eighties, including Andrew Young, Jesse Jackson, and Joseph Lowery, are all ministers of various

Protestant faiths. Even such leaders as Vernon Jordan, who are not ministers, always prefer to use the pulpit to launch their messages, because they know it will provide them with a large coherent audience of faithful listeners.

A few questions still remain regarding the typically religious aspects of the movement. How have the Christian and Protestant religions of the black communities been affected by the tendency of Protestant churches to splinter and spawn new churches, by the new material that has found its way to America along with the recent Caribbean immigrants, and by the formation of new cults? Although it is exceedingly difficult to treat these questions as one, the answer may be found by analyzing—as we will later—the relationships that have formed between the black churches, the large American mainstream churches, and the new cults.

The Catholic Church has played a part in black religiosity thanks to its powerful organization, its persuasive national strength and international scope, and the good quality of its schools and universities. Some qualified and socially mobile black individuals and groups have turned to Catholicism, but this has done nothing to alter the overall makeup of the black community. The black community continues to be irreversibly Protestant. The American nature and setting of the day-to-day problems blacks must face make it unlikely that they would ever embrace a religion whose historical background is so different from their own. The feeling that keeps America's blacks bound to those origins can only be matched by Protestant nostalgia for the early settlements. No mere sentimental attachments, these are a society's response to the problems inherent in a lifestyle, a geographical setting, and a shared history. The Protestant church was the original venue for this adventure, and it remains the most suitable vehicle for this response, thanks to its heritage of civic and community service and its pragmatic willingness to fit in with surrounding circumstances.

The Baptist churches and evangelical preaching should be given special attention in discussing black religiosity. With their emphasis on redemption, revival, miracles, and instant salvation, it was only natural that these movements establish roots among the relatively poor population living in small town and rural settings, well removed from the places where political decision making occurs or where the news is made. Blacks form a substantial proportion of these populations. As it is well known, some of the white evangelical and Baptist groups are precisely those most susceptible to racial fear, anxiety, and prejudice regarding the black-white "difference." Thus although initial relations between black worshipers and the Baptist and evangelical movements were quite solid, they soon began to deteriorate into de facto segregation. Of course, any two religious trends that share such strength and dimension are bound to overlap continuously, but today most Baptist and evangelical churches would have to be implicitly defined as "predominantly white" or "predominantly black," with the result that there are two Baptist churches and two evangelical movements. Any tendency to increase the size of minority membership has been motivated by religious rather than social or civic circumstances, so that integration in these churches does not affect the separation that may still exist in other aspects of life.

As for black influence on predominantely white American churches, the phenomenon may be best appraised by analyzing some of the white churches and cults and the ways they have evolved in recent years. Most new evangelical churches show recognizable features of the black tradition, the passionate hope and the total abandonment to faith that typify black religious culture. This is true even in the cases where separation has been most tenacious. Furthermore, black religion has noticeably affected the civic and social behavior of other churches, including the Jewish and Catholic faiths. The black churches have stressed the moral values of civil rights, previously an area of far less concern for many white churches.

Relations between the black churches and new religions and cults are of special interest in this contest. The first of the new American cults was the Mormon faith, now just over a century and a half old. Then there were all the movements, groups, sects, and cults that began to proliferate after the fifties and particularly in the sixties, ranging from Reverend Moon's Unification Church to such factions as the Children of God and the Jesus Children.

The Mormon church explicitly forbade blacks to participate in any form of leadership in the church, and still discourages their membership in the congregation. A strong local sect, the Mormons have a powerful and well-organized church governed by discretion bordering on the cult of secrecy. They show no interest in expansion or proliferation. The Mormons have expanded the Protestant tendency to form an exclusive club, and they believe that salvation can only be attained if this club is kept free of nonmembers, as defined at the sect's inception. Some of these features were passed along to newer cults.

It seems the new cults have concentrated on the middle or upper-middle classes, where blacks are poorly represented. But the "white" birth of these cults was not intentional; it was an inevitable consequence of the socioeconomic status of the groups in search of a new religion. Now it would be unthinkable for the new religious sects of America to change their stance with respect to the black masses, but many of these movements show clear signs of nostalgia, even envy, for the way blacks participate in their churches. The new white cults are proof of the way black religion has affected white groups in search of identity and an image, although it would be difficult to assess the conscious extent of this influence. There may be a powerful need for aggregation underlying the secret and segregated nature of the new cults, which were fated not to be "with the blacks" but "like the blacks."

Obviously, an enormous difference exists between the large cities—where relations in the community and thus in the church tend to disintegrate—and the original small town and rural settlements. Nevertheless, the organization, participation, and commitment that characterize black religion still seem to offer the strongest and most solid model for community solidarity.

Undoubtedly, these churches are still among the most fervid and active areas of worship in the United Staes today.

REVIVAL AND THE QUEST FOR MIRACLES

America has often been swept by the tempestuous winds of various religious revivals, each of which has left scars or signs of change. Typically, revivals are fueled by emotion or existing tension rather than by theological content. Because of this, they can easily rage out of control, igniting millions of people with their appeals to the irrational aspects of faith. Fundamentalist and conservative on the one hand, egalitarian and utopian on the other, they include the Billy Graham-type international celebrities and the circuit preacher, the large cities and the rural backroads, the social aggregation of brotherhood and the racial alienation of segregation. All these movements share the exaltation and magical character of the revival, with its crucial feature, the promise and expectation of miracles. Whether the miracle is an unexpected awakening of faith or the healing of an incurable affliction, it is bound to appear more frequently as the cultural conditions of the group become simpler and more elementary.

In this way, the miracle takes the place of the liturgy, which has always played a modest role in Protestant faiths; likewise, it replaces God's presence in Holy Communion, a sacrament the Catholic Church shares with very few Protestant denominations. Thanks to the wafer, the Catholic Church has been able to keep the miracle out of its mass gatherings, but the evangelical revivals resemble such large Catholic events as the Eucharist congresses enough to warrant a comparison.

The Catholic Church has moved away from public and spectacular performance of the miracle, in the last two centuries, considering it a thing of the past and out of place, although not impossible. Diversely, evangelicalism has embraced the miracle with steadily increasing and spreading passion, tending more and more often to emphasize blind faith and celebration. The

Catholic Church can still reward its followers with the wealth of its ritual and the powerful charisma of its leaders—the scene that comes to mind is John Paul II's nighttime parade before a capacity crowd in New York's huge Yankee Stadium. And it can give them the specific object of faith: the presence of God.

The evangelical movement would seem to result from the Protestant church's failures to invest its liturgical events with the same kind of tension. A need arose to fill the gap with the immediate and absolute verification of the miracle. Of course, this sort of proof is a matter of faith, so that the problem of logical credibility is overcome once collective fervor has crossed the threshold of absolute dedication.

Thus to risk an analogy with Freudian interpretation, the evangelical movement seems to derive from an unconscious "Sacrament envy." A great many revival movements are characterized by rites and ritual activities that have gradually acquired the same value as the Sacrament. These features may be derivations, imitations, or even the results of "envy," but that has not stopped the American evangelical movements from gathering enough strength first to undermine traditional distinctions among the various Protestant churches and then, much to the surprise of the sociologists of religion, to attack the staunchly defended bastions of the Catholic institution. The outcome has been the American Catholic Church's new moderate policy, which tends to accept the "spiritual value" of some religious revivals because they represent a reawakening of religious desire and the search for Christ. This statement may imply an attempt to exert some sort of control over the performance and proliferation of these events. Clearly, the Catholic approval is conditional, and thus it is subtle proof that the slow hemorrhage of Catholics who have evidently begun to participate in the revivals is being countered by a warning to keep these movements within acceptable limits for those Catholics. Because the evangelical movements are also gigantic commercial ventures reminiscent of the largest rock concerts, this warning could assume great importance. Today it is still too early to calculate proportions in Catholic-evangelical relations. Certainly the American Catholic Church has shown no signs of weakness, but this is the first time it has ever come to terms with a Protestant movement, and, in this case, with the least rigorous form of Protestant faith.

The evangelical revival is always conservative and intolerant, even when it seems to accept the Gospels' most fervent appeals for solidarity. This is because mobilization of the masses is always an unconscious challenge to the absent; it draws the line between the faithful and the infidel and must inevitably conclude with one call for exaltation and another for indictment. This gives rise to tempestuous and often irrational moral campaigns that tend to spread through the most unexpected channels, ranging from the courts to the schools.

The evangelical revival is only the visible tip of an organizational network whose continually improving links can affect every sector of public and social life. One example is the Christian Yellow Pages, a business directory that lists all the "Christian" firms with which the "faithful" are supposed to conduct their business, thus excluding or implictly segregating "non-Christians," meaning those who do not belong to one of the movement's various factions.

Once again we are faced with the exclusion so typical of America's Protestant roots. In a country that is a mosaic of diversities harmonized by tolerance, this project poses a formidable threat, although the rulings of several courts have blocked it for some time. However, evangelicalism seems to go beyond the letter of the law in interfering with public and political life, and it thus can influence the legislator even beofre his or her election. During the 1980 primaries and the 1984 presidential campaign, several candidates, particularly conservatives, made frequent use of phrases and slogans borrowed from the evangelical movement. This explicit religious commitment has even contaminated the Catholic community, provoking new militancy in such areas as abortion and suddenly endangering a whole array of liberal positions thought to be final and routinely accepted since the beginning of the sixties.

Another similarity among these movements is the way they

shift the cultural and social reference point to small town and rural areas, where evangelical mobilization is more likely to succeed. By isolating the "sinful" big cities and universities, urban culture, scientific research, and liberalism are placed under constant siege. In addition, the delicate component of racism in the evangelist movements is another serious element which cannot be overlooked: the evangelicals, because of their aspiration to a pure Christian society, are silently, even unconsciously, anti-Semitic, and their followers are recruited almost exclusively from the white population. When the political implications of the movement have become clearer, its racial overtones will come to light as well. There is no doubt that the American Jewish community, despite its present political conservative policies and links with the "new Christian" political groups, is nourishing doubts and anxiety about an emerging wave of "pure Christian America" preachers. If evangelicalism is analyzed as a religious phenomenon there is little space for cultural analysis, given the elementary character of the movement, with its impassioned and incontestable behaviors. In this sense, we must look at the movement from the social and political point of view. Evangelicalism may be culturally primitive and theologically simplistic, but at the same time it values participation in civic affairs. Thus its potential influence covers enormous ground, although this appears to be overlooked by the most sophisticated sectors of American politics and by the intellectual community.

THE MANY FACES OF AMERICAN CATHOLICISM

If we compare it with each of the Protestant denominations and not with Protestantism as a whole, the most powerful, well-organized, and largest religious institution in the United States today is the Catholic Church. Its structure is more highly evolved than any others; it is endowed with a glamorous international stature; has a rich and ancient liturgy, which is made even more spectacular by the austere standards of the United States, a country with little ceremony and no royal tradition. Catholicism alone has a pope, thought to be the living representative of Christ on earth, and it is the only religion that ritualizes every one of life's fundamental acts from birth to death through sanction and celebration of the Sacraments.

This list of the typical features of American Catholicism also implicitly indicates the type of historical and social problems that have confronted the Catholic Church in the United States. First, there is the connotation of ecumenism and internationalism in a culture preoccupied with drawing boundary lines and defining membership and loyalty to its own way of life. Above all there is the historical handicap of American Catholicism, which came to this country as the "foreign" religion of immigrant minorities and was forced, after centuries of its own hegemony, power, and dominance, to bow to the Protestant culture that had already taken control in America. When it arrived here, Catholicism was identified with poor, "inferior" communities whose climb out of those conditions was destined to be long and painful. And unlike other reglions, which could blend in with a vision shared by all, Catholicism already possessed features and values which were nonnegotiable, unmodifiable, and unable to fit the surroundings and the times. What is more, it was firmly linked to its own Roman origins, which were "un-American" per se. In 1984, President Reagan's decision to appoint a U.S. ambassador to the Vatican did not go unchallenged and, while finally approved by Congress, stirred passionate debates and strong opposition.

Catholicism has come to America three times, and while each wave originated in a different cultural background, all three shared the status of inferiority. The first arrival was with the poor Irish masses; the second with the poor Italian masses; the third with a vast and less clearly defined onslaught from extremely different historical and cultural backgrounds throughout Central and Latin America. The third wave has brought additional infusions of local religion, in the form of magic cults.

Thus the American Catholic Church has a history of foreign

relations with other cultures and domestic relations among its own different branches. Both these histories have abounded with troubles and tensions, some of which still have to be resolved. But there have been the great successes, beginning with the rise out of a state of inferiority surpassed only by that of the blacks. The domestic history of American Catholicism developed along with the three waves of immigration. Each wave met its own resistance and grew accordingly, and the different conditions show how well the Church has adjusted to find its place in history.

When the Irish came to the New World, they had one advantage none of the other Catholic immigrants would share: they spoke the language. On the other hand, they were burdened with the dramatic historical disadvantage of identification with a religion that represented an open wound in Anglo-Saxon culture. The struggle to adapt could not have been harder, but the Irish had a head start, thanks to the group's intense association with its religion, established for reasons of defense preceding emigration to America. The Irish were further helped by the arrival en masse of entire communities with their clergymen. Thus although they faced the same severe obstacles to adaptation shared by many other immigrant groups, they were fortunate enough to be a coherent group whose identification with its church and priests could not be threatened. Because of these circumstances, the Irish clergy later established irreversible predominance over successive immigrant arrivals, almost to the point of colonization and subordination.

The Italians came to America under different conditions, first because the immigrants were from sharply contrasting regional and cultural backgrounds and then because the Church played a different role in their lives. Compared to the Irish, the Italians had only weak generic ties to their religion, so that in America they were branded less for their Catholicism than for their poverty and ethnic identity; in addition, they had to overcome the language barrier. Most of the Italian immigrants came from southern Italy, where relations between peasants and the

Church had never been as close as those between the Irish Church and its community. Furthermore, such skilled immigrants as the weavers of Prato, who had benefitted from better cultural conditions, arrived—at the end of the nineteenth century—with a secular and socialist point of view that made them far more sympathetic to the humanitarian solidarity of the Jews on New York's Lower East Side than to the Irish parish.

So Italian Catholicism in America has had a history of progressive recovery from an initial state of division and isolation. It is important to remember that the Italian clergy only participated in immigration from the sidelines, given the unique social structure of the original community. Furthermore, each immigrant group brought along the vivid memory of a tradition or a saint which kept it focused upon a local fragment of Catholicism, thereby discouraging a coherent or dogmatic viewpoint. Fresh from a country where religion had always coincided with authority, the Ialians were skeptical that the Church could serve as a defense and a shelter. So the difficult road ahead became a two-way thoroughfare, with one lane heading forward to assimilation into the new society and the other going backward to the rediscovery and reconstruction of a religious identity that had been hazy, if not altogether nonexistent, when they arrived in the New World. American culture soon made it quite clear to the newcomers that membership in a "club" was essential, and the only club open to the Italians was the Catholic Church. But the price of admission was subordination to the Irish clergy. Still today, with over twenty million Italian-American Catholics, there are a handful of bishops of Italian ancestry and only one cardinal.

Thanks to these circumstances, Italians had an entirely different relationship with their Church. Where ethnic self-affirmation was involved the ties were strong, but when it came to daily worship the Italians lagged are behind the Irish. More concerned with loyalty to their local origins or to a special saint, the Italians conserved their peasant traditions and popular culture. This experience created a black hole in the history of im migration, for with no clear religious identification or strong Church affiliation, the Italians suffered longer and more deeply than other groups. A case in point was Pope John Paul II's visit to the United States in 1979. Although the Italians proudly out-number the Irish in the New York area's Catholic Church, they were excluded from all the most important activities, with the exception of the pope's brief visit to a Brooklyn parish house. Not one Italian-American clergyman had the stature or title to appear alongside the Holy Father.

The third wave of Catholicism in America has been shaped by profoundly disparate Latin American groups: Puerto Ricans, Central Americans, Mexicans, Caribbeans. These immigrants have been subjected to the double subordination to the Irish and the Italians; in turn, they have infiltrated the Church with native magic cults spawned by their unique history and by the survival of African traditions. This is the high point of conflict between the original Catholic tradition of the "full" church and the "empty" Protestant church mentioned earlier. But since the Catholic religion first landed on American shores, Irish lead-ership has molded the Church into the most rigid and "Prot-estant" form of Catholicism in the world. This can be detected in a hesitancy to strike pragmatic compromises with the coun-try's institutions, in greater moral stringency, and in a desire for more tangible signs of faith, such as wearing the black mark of Ash Wednesday penitence on one's forehead for an entire day, as a declaration of faith and an implicit challenge to non-Catholics. None of these features can be found in European Catholicism, particularly in its Italian form.

On the other hand, this Protestantization has gone hand in hand with construction of a solid inner framework that has al-lowed American Catholicism to become a center of unmatched power. Today the Catholic Church actively pursues its policy of relations with other religious denominations. Keeping a watchful eye on ethnic divisions, it has calmly absorbed the re-ligious organizations of Eastern European origin. On the home front, it has established firm lines of practical and moral collab-oration with American Christianity, often sharing stands on issues of public morality ranging from abortion to pornography, although carefully avoiding such typically American Protestant issues as evolution theory vs. creationism. The Church has devoted particular attention to relations with the Jewish community, which shares its position of historical discrimination and social values, and with the black community, for whom the Catholic Church's stigma of apparent lack of interest is counterbalanced by its uninvolvement in the ugly vicissitudes of racism. The election of a Polish pope has liberated American Catholicism from the onus of seeming too Roman, and the recent international popularity of that pope has tempered the other potential danger, that a "foreign" influence might contaminate an American church. Now all the conditions exist for the Catholic Church to exert its authority, prestige, and influence; indeed, it has been conducting a cautious but skillful campaign to expand its areas of influence.

As we have seen, American Catholicism has accommodated three great onslaughts from Ireland, Italy, and Latin America. No church but this one, with its firmly established hierarchy, theology, and organization, could ever have reconciled three groups of such estranged and conflicting heritage. It was pointed out above that the Irish dominate the church hierarchy. Its earlier experience with Protestantism helped the Irish community toward some understanding and even affinity. The Protestant accent on individual awareness has inspired a certain sense of self-disciplined austerity; this is much more noticeable among the Irish than among the Italians, and it is altogether absent among Latin Americans. We have seen that the Irish have dominated church hierarchy partly because the clergy immigrated alongside its congregation, who could speak the language of the new country and were carefully organized. However, in the meantime the Italians have steadily become the most faithful worshipers. America has inverted Catholicism's original roots, so that some of the Italian immigrants who arrived here with so little sense of religious practice have now become the most scrupulous observers.

As for the third wave of immigrants, the many Latin American groups have come from even greater poverty and cultural confusion than their predecessors. But they have arrived in America in an age of awareness about civil rights and strongly monitored the media. This has allowed these immigrants to preserve their heritage and traditions, with all their color, fervor, superstition, and ritual. In addition, they have been able to keep their language, so that they have immediately coagulated into an antagonistic force capable of defending its rights. In the sixties, the boycott instigated by California's Mexican fruit pickers under the leadership of Catholic labor organizer Cesar Chavez was accorded only slightly less national prestige than Martin Luther King's movement. Nothing of the sort ever happened to the Italians, whose church has now become a consecration of complete absorption into the disciplined and industrious ranks of the middle class.

But although, for instance, the almost total dearth of relations between the Spanish and Italian Catholic communities attests to a potential for separation and profound diversity, church leadership always manages to transform this threat into an advantage over other churches. American Catholicism is at once the establishment and the protest movement; it represents accepted values as well as progress toward new rights, affirmation, recognition, and a continual demand for the acknowledgment of national and local character. These contradictions constantly reinforce the moral and political power of the institution, so that Catholicism has a unique place in American history and society. For these reasons, it might be said that the headquarters of world Catholicism are in Rome but its strength and mass support are in the United States.

JUDAISM COMES TO AMERICA

The conditions under which America's Jewish communities formed were relatively similar to those described for Catholicism: many groups diversified by their national and local characteristics were able to weave themselves into a coherent religious movement blessed with a deep sense of solidarity. The success of American Jewish culture seems all the more extraordinary given the lack of a centralized hierarchy and the modest size of the militant force. The establishment of Judaism in America took place under several other unique conditions which have no precedent in history. Only the blacks met greater discrimination in America than the Jews, who were more fortunate than the blacks beacuse they were free. But Jews were cursed by the fact that their definition by exclusion had already been sanctioned by European culture.

When Judaism reached the New World, it came in an incredible variety of national origins and social levels. The desperately poor Russians and East Europeans joined the relatively wealthy and thoroughly educated West Europeans, who possessed a higher level of European culture than any group since the Anglo-Saxons of colonial days. These two Jewish communities have reinforced each other continually—the latest examples being refugees first from Nazi Europe and then from the Soviet Union—and Judaism soon achieved a degree of inner solidarity matched by no other American community. In the New World, with its onus of discrimination but blessing of opportunity, the Jewish community used its original segregated status as a springboard from which to form an immense reserve of quality and talent that has gone on to shine in many if not all arenas of American success.

The initial restrictions of segregation, a tradition of isolation, and a history of persecution have helped to keep any internal strife, whether caused by nationality and language or as a result of different religious traditions and degrees of orthodoxy, from having the same importance it once had among the orginal settlements of the conservative Orthodox sects. The Hasidic communities in New York's Williamsburg district have almost no relations with the intellectuals of Western European cultural roots, but solidarity still unites the diamond cutter with the scientific researcher and amalgamates all the vastly different groups with bonds that even the Catholic Church cannot match History and tradition have played opposite roles in American Judasism and Protestantism, with the result that Judaism has increasingly valued internal understanding, awareness, recognition, and cooperation instead of separation into splinter groups and ever-changing denominations. Hence the Protestant irritation with Jewish culture, which is repeatedly and unjustly accused of controlling the news media and business. Inversely, Jewish relations with Catholicism have always been good, or at least better, because both culture groups have grown from similar degrees of exclusion, and perhaps because they have both come to represent a "federation" uniting many historical and national roots into one faith.

It is no coincidence that Italians and Jews fought side by side throughout the entire first stage of labor organization in America, just as it is no accident that relations, even family ties, between these two groups formed the closest interethnic ties that have ever existed in the country at the beginning of the century. But this was only true as long as the Italians were not entirely absorbed into the Irish-dominated Catholic church, because the process of Protestantization mentioned earlier took Catholicism a few steps backward toward a certain degree of sectarianism, which extended to the Italian community. And in fact, when it came time to fight for civil rights, only the Jewish community offered group support for the cause of black emancipation. Italian participation was limited to individuals, even though some, like Viola Liuzzo, were among the movement's victims, and others, like Father Groppi, were among its leaders.

The overtones of fundamentalism and liberal reform that have continually characterized American public life have also profoundly influenced Jewish culture. Indeed, American Judaism is not one homogeneous cultural entity, nor could it ever be one, given the vitality and disparity of options it has to offer. Each of these different groups has been shaped over the ages, with whole geneological lines of the Jewish culture split since long before the Diaspora. Even such firmly rooted Jewish traits as liberalism or political militancy do not indicate the presence of a compact social structure. But every time the group's identity is threatened from without, it reacts by reinforcing the loose cultural and historical bonds that unite all these groups into one confederation.

Among all the American ethnic groups, only the blacks and the Jews seem to have learned that the best defense against external danger is allegiance despite diversity. But the blacks have been plagued for a long time by the endemic separatism of the Protestant culture, whereas Jewish groups have used the options offered by America's special situation to establish the religion's most authoritative and coherent leadership since the Diaspora. Perhaps for this reason, no other group identifies quite so strongly with its dual status, and each individual feels equally American and Jewish. Furthermore, this duality has only apparently been shaken by ongoing relations between the American Jewish community and the state of Israel. True, a few American Jews have left their homeland to live in Israel, and almost no American Jew would withdraw support for Israel even while recognizing her occasional political errors. But to harbor doubts about the American Jews' loyalty to the political institutions of the United States would be to ignore the history and the moral image of a community that now plays an incontestably major role in the American way of life.

THE NEW SECTS AND "SECULAR CULTS"

The schismatic nature of Protestantism makes it impossible to list all the new sects and cults which became known in the last two decades. But despite their relatively fluid structure and susceptibility to dramatic short-term change, they all share several points of reference.

Churches and Sects Based on Secrecy and Conspiracy. Churches and sects have embellished a common core of fundamentalism with a wide range of new features. Unlike the

Protestant churches that generated them, they have allowed ideology and political trends to infiltrate their organizations and they have returned to the charismatic leader, in reaction to a culture that has always preferred self-government to strong power symbols. But "conspiracy" does not necessarily imply negative, illegal connotations: here it is more a physiological characteristic. "Conspiratory" is the best way to describe churches and sects that practice self-exclusion, self-segregation, and self-imprisonment as a result of deep mistrust toward the general society originally shared by all the members of the new cult and later kept alive through various forms of imposition. This diffidence extends to government, social structure, commonly accepted behavior, and the prevailing morality. All these characteristics are possessed by the churches of disillusionment born toward the end of the sixties, but few sects have matched the paranoia and persecution mania of the tragic People's Temple, led by Jim Jones in San Francisco and Guayana, and the love for secrecy cultivated by the church founded and presided over ty the Reverend Moon.

Continually Evolving Evangelical Movements. These churches are an ongoing reproduction of Protestant culture's original seed, as manifested in preaching, proselytism, the reawakening, baptism, and the experience of rebirth. With their forceful emphasis on the miracle, such movements can draw upon endless amounts of vitality and tension as their founding cultures are repeatedly affirmed and deformed. But their evangelicalism and "new birth" are constantly exposed to contamination by different features of other new American faiths.

Neo-Christian Proselytizing Movements. Such groups as the Children of God and the Jesus Children have borrowed rigid elements from the Catholic teachings, including the message of salvation to be gained through evocation of Jesus, the son of God. They have combined these elements with traditional forms of Protestant association and with the secrecy cult of the conspiracy churches. It would be hard to measure the impact such groups have had, but it is not unreasonable to assume that the repercussions reach farther than has generally been thought.

Conservative Fundamentalism. A coalition of diverse offshoots from the Baptist and evangelical churches, this movement's cultural epicenter is far removed from the big cities and firmly entrenched in localism, with its tenacious ideal of a "pure America." A shared program of blanket rejection has consolidated these sects into a front. Although the movement seems to march behind a banner of religious anxiety, there may be even stronger sociological, economic, and cultural roots at the bottom of its rejections, which have included any number of issues. There is the battle between rural and urban values; there is a longing for the past vs. the hard reality of the present; there is a demand for protection of the middle class, whose place halfway between the rich and the poor has been threatened by recent crises and recessions which have tended, in their drastic and simplistic way, to wipe out class distinctions. There is also the protest against permissiveness as generated by the sixties. So the conservative fundamentalist movement has grown out of a constellation of "anti" campaigns: against sin and secular humanism; against the blasphemous cities; against the cultural establishment's tolerance of sin, and thus against culture itself; against the news media and mass communications, and thus in favor of censorship; against abortion, divorce, homosexuality, and the liberal interpretation of civil rights.

What emerges is a mixture of general religious themes and specific political objectives. This corresponds with the movement's progressive expansion in both the religious and political worlds, as well as with the affirmation of such fronts as the Moral Majority, which came into the limelight during the 1980 presidential campaign. Because the movement arose and consolidated on the basis of an appeal for a state of purity thought to belong to the past and inherent in original values thought to have disappeared, the front is fiercely conservative. It may only have been a political tactic to enlarge the manifesto of conservative fundamentalism by adding the call for life-or-death defense of Israel (the movement calls itself Zionist) and the passionate campaign to increase United States military spending. The first of these two themes may appear to compensate for the risk of anti-Semitism inevitably present in any fundamentalist-evangelical coalition. The call to arms may be the political expression of a new religious fervor, in which esteem for "age-old values" would naturally include defense of "what is right." Finally, almost every position espoused by the vast conglomeration of conservative fundamentalist groups has opposed the religious and secular liberalism that predominated in the sixties.

The movement has always been white, although this has occurred spontaneously rather than according to premeditated plans. An overwhelming majority of its followers come from the middle class, live outside or far from the big cities, and are stubbornly hostile to the philosophy behind American liberalism, particularly as expressed over the past two decades, and to the consequences it has created. For these reasons, the new fundamentalism is alienated from the mainstream churches, although it has made some inroads into the Catholic Church, especially after John Paul II's revival of the antiabortion commitment. It has also affected American Judaism, arousing sympathy with its support for Israel, and creating suspicion with its intense neo-Christian sectarianism.

The "Secular Cults". These groups do possess some ecclesiastical overtones, and they assign a significant role to cult objects derived from religious, psychological, and therapeutical syncretism. One typical example is Synanon, which began as a way to help former drug addicts find salvation through cohabitation; another is est, or Erhardt Seminar Training, a school for the self-gratification of a financially prosperous but psychologically frail upper-middle class in search of its cultural identity. The first example serves as a reminder that the conspiratory structure also extends to groups that are not openly religious. The second indicates a culture that has emphasized the more superficial and immediate needs that religious practice fulfills— i.e. the passage from troublesome reality to the well-being of compensatory values—and then transformed them into training. Werner Erhardt is the pseudonym used by an enterprising individual who has set up a program of costly "seminars" for which participants deprived of sleep and all other comforts are forced to "accept and recognize themselves" through slapdash and even brutal application of several marginal techniques borrowed from different interpretations of psychoanalysis. Ostensibly open and cooperative, est actually shares many features with the conspiracy cults, such as training its members to be invulnerable to criticism and scornful of the debate surrounding their movement.

Another interesting example is Joseph Granville, whose business newsletter goes out from a small Florida town to thousands of subscribers, exerting extraordinary effects on the ups and downs of Wall Street. On one December day in 1980, the New York Stock Exchange suddenly plummeted more than twenty-five points—to the astonishment of trading experts— because Granville's publication had issued its readers an unexpected order to sell. Such immediate obedience testifies to Granville's charismatic influence over his readers. Whether he is addressing his audience from the podium or from the pages with which he has flooded America, Granville's language strangely resembles preaching, with the same inspirational overtones and theatricality of religious revivals of the liturgy and the Sacraments. Granville does not hesitate to refer to God and faith. But apart from psychological synchronization with the same communication techniques, the real affinity between Granville's operations and the religion they so vividly evoke is the inspiration and absolutism of this self-elected spokesman for the truth, who in reality is no more than an investment expert. Even though he has never established the explicit identity of a church for his disciples, everything that motivates and occurs to them is directly comparable to the relations that exist between a sect and its followers, and it is reasonable to think that Granville has not overlooked this likeness.

Something very similar has been achieved by the group of political and electoral fund raisers led by one of conservative America's most famed celebrities, direct-mail wizard Richard Viguerie. The "letters" Viguerie often uses as a means of communication with his public, as well as his books and public statements, abound with ecclesiastical jargon, the shared-inspiration motif, and the writer's personal charisma, so that the organizational setting of Viguerie's operations is clearly shifted from the political to the religious sphere. Once again an invocation of the truth becomes a challenge to enemy values, pitting the indisputable against the contestable, the wholesome against the sick, and the desirable against the dangerous.

All of these characters—Werner Erhardt of est, Joseph Granville the investment adviser, Richard Viguerie the political organizer—are secular leaders with no personal religious motivations or spiritual causes to espouse. Each has attained undeniable success, thanks to easily perceivable charisma and widely publicized practical goals, and each has chosen to use religious and spiritual inspiration to conduct operations that are anything but theological. Nor are these unconscious imitations or simple tricks. They are the result of shrewd calculation. The fact that "inspired," religious-sounding language can mobilize more people more readily than the language that would be appropriate for each of these three areas—psychological training, financial decision making, and political organization—is one more sign of America's current cultural climate, which comes on the heels of the disappointments of the sixties and seventies. It seems there is a collective need for certainty and faith, something like the craving for a father figure psychologists so often find to be the key to interpreting anxious behavior.

The Eastern Cults. Vedanta, Hare Krishna, the different interpretations of Buddhism and Zen, related meditation techniques, and other movements and cults inspired by Oriental religion represent a separate category for examination. Careful analysis would show that there are differences between training programs and religious groups, as well as between vocations that take over a whole life, changing it radically, and cultural viewpoints that only inspire certain behavioral patterns such as abstentionism, reflection, and meditation. And yet the Oriental religious beliefs and the spiritual demands that are eventually met by the Eastern conception of life go back to roots that clearly differ from all the other trends mentioned above. They indicate the presence of underlying tensions and polarizations that ought to find expression in cultural and political terms, but emerge as religious choices instead.

Indeed, it might be said that the whole trend toward Oriental religion is an indirect reflection of unfulfilled liberal needs, just as the neo-Christian churches, new fundamentalism, new evangelicalism, and the secular cults that use ecclesiastical language seem to satisfy conservative needs. This conception is supported by numerous historical and cultural indications. To begin with, the Eastern religions were first introduced to America by liberals, or at least by groups with no specific political affiliation, but certainly closer to the liberal mind.

Two recently published books give some insight into the human and psychological conditions that set the stage for the turn to Eastern religions. In *The Guru and His Disciple*, Christopher Isherwood describes the experience of Vedanta in the Hollywood of 1939, with war around the corner and hostility to Nazism already on the rise. Later, Robert Pirsig's *Zen and the Art of Motorcycle Maintenance* was a best seller, filling part of the gap left by the depressing Vietnam and Watergate years. Eastern spirituality took its place in the American cultural landscape as a follow-up to political commitment, an attempt to establish wider horizons in order to compensate for the disappointment of failure. And indeed, a great many of the cultural and militant resources of the sixties were later channeled toward Oriental religions. But it would be wrong to interpret these religions as recycling plants or temporary storage dumps for misplaced energies. The requirements of this type of religious belief are every bit as stringent as those of any other church. Indeed, they may be the strictest of them all, because they entail drastic changes in life-style and personal relations, and once the decision to embrace the new creed has been made it is almost impossible to revert to previous conditions. Even when the new religious faith is limited to simple techniques, such as meditation or the concentration that make it possible to achieve wider and deeper vision, the follower is unlikely to be able to retrace his footsteps. Once perfect example is the "culture" acquired by the Beatles, John Lennon in particular. Despite the brevity of his actual exposure to the teachings of Maharishi Yogi, Lennon never rejected Eastern spiritualism for the rest of his life. The aura of celebration that surrounded his own death still bore the signs of the unique life-death correlations he had learned from the Hindu preachings of the Maharishi. In the end, even those who practice Eastern religion from the sidelines are exposed to its respect for abstention, which makes it impossible or at least arduous to participate in any form of political militancy or practical commitment.

There are two other cultural groups that should be considered under this heading, despite the high degree of activism that characterizes them: the ecological movements and the groups that tend to relate a different outlook on life to improved relations with one's body and thus with food. Both these movements are based upon a link between the spiritual and the physical or upon abstention as an expression of respect for nature and the environment. Despite their limitless forms and combinations, they are just as affected by Oriental culture as they are opposed to typical Western efficiency and organization.

These underlying motivations for the decision to find one's spirituality in the East are far more important than the exotic costumes and rituals often associated with such new forms of non-Western religion as the Hare Krishna cult. For instance, they explain why the intelligence and creativity of liberal America have seemed and will probably continue in the predictable future to seem exhausted, whereas the neo-Christian conservative religious camp is bursting with wealth and vitality. Many of the energies that were once expressed in liberal and progressive viewpoints are now oriented, both psychologically and culturally, toward abstention.

So there are good reasons to say that American liberalism has been channeled into a deadening private and individual care for the self, at the same time that the conservative cause's new interpretation of the Old and New Testaments has provided the robust strength needed to take over the American political scene. However, it must never be forgotten that religious rigor in America is not founded upon philosophical precepts or absolute dogmas, nor can it ever become an ideological rock or an eternal foundation. It is not enough to assess the fluidity of these characteristics: it is every bit as important to evaluate the contradictions and tensions still rumbling beneath ground that has only apparently resettled.

TWO

The War of the Churches

O<small>NLY</small> a few weeks after Ronald Reagan was triumphantly elected to the White House, the religious wing of the new conservative front presented its manifesto. The coalition known as the Moral Majority began mobilization for its "war on sin" in New York, where Reverend Jerry Falwell met with representatives of the major television networks and the leading newspapers of America on February 5, 1981. Although the encounter was calm and orderly, the climate was anything but cool, and the media were quick to recognize the looming threat.

A. Bartlett Giamatti, President of Yale University, defined the danger on September 1 of the same year in an address to the student body. "A self-proclaimed 'Moral Majority' and its satellite or client groups, cunning in the use of a native blend of old intimidation and new technology, threaten the values of our pluralistic society." Giamatti went on to say that this "maw of 'morality' " is aligned with rising anti-Semitism, a burgeoning Ku Klux Klan, and a program to boycott "un-Christian" television programs. Claiming to be the caretakers of the truth, these people attack anyone who dares to present a different version of reality.

Meanwhile, Falwell and his Moral Majority had also come to the attention of *Jewish Weekly*, an influential magazine published by the Jewish community of New York; an American Jewish Committee trend analysis;

Arthur Hertzberg, vice-president of the World Jewish Congress; Mayor Andrew Young of Atlanta; William Sloane Coffin, senior pastor of New York's Riverside Church; and the evangelist-preacher Billy Graham.

The problem was political, because the neo-Christian churches that inspired the Moral Majority considered themselves centers for the kind of conservatism that had rallied around the new administration. And it was religious, because it involved relations between the intransigent fundamentalist impetus of the new churches and the spirit of tolerance inherent in traditional religions. A thread of discomfort runs between Falwell's headquarters and the Catholic Church; between neoevangelism and the Baptist churches; between white and black neo-Christians; between leaders championed by Reagan and the Republican Party he has renewed and those who follow such pastors as Andrew Young, Jackson or William Sloane Coffin, whose cultural roots lie in the sixties and close to the leadership of Martin Luther King. Relations between the Moral Majority and America's Jewish organizations are more strained, as a result of the conflict between the Moral Majority's "total" support of Israel and its neo-Christian fervor, which has been in the past traditionally anti-Semitic.

All of this is interwoven and confused with day-to-day political events, the media's presentation of its cherished personalities—and Jerry Falwell is certainly a member of this group—and constantly changing national and international tensions. But the truly new element on the American scene is this: real confrontation and a respectable portion of the political debate occur among the churches. The origins and profound causes for today's antagonisms and alliances are to be found within and among the church-inspired organizations. The political parties are caught between the desire to avoid religious issues (such as abortion or prayers in the school) and the evidence that religious issues are a relevant part of the political debate.

THE ORIGINS OF NEO-CHRISTIAN FUNDAMENTALISM

Is there a specifically American reason for this new brand of political confrontation which is formed and transformed by the churches instead of by the media and political action?

Undoubtedly, several aspects of America's democratic culture and tradition have hindered clear definition of the country's political forces, thereby allowing them to overlap and intertwine. The system of election to the House or the Senate is individual electoral districts establishes strong ties between the representative and his constituency. Historical and regional coalitions continually disrupt party policy and sometimes redesign interparty boundaries. The legislative process is continually intercepted by ephemeral but influential coalitions on such specific issues as ecology, taxation, and monetary policy and these separations frequently alter the wide and shifting gaps between liberal and conservative camps, constantly changing the moderate middle ground that generally represents the majority. When European observers attempt to translate American politics in terms of their own cultures, they would do well to keep track of the liberal and conservative poles, rather than to analyze party positions, which might bring American politics closer to the European interpretation of ideology but would often be misleading, because of the broad margins for variation and pragmatic adjustment.

Public activity draws upon the good common sense of the business world, where obedience to the rules of the game is required. Yet often those rules are stretched to accommodate the most convenient position. If the people and groups that determine America's politics frequently appear to be incoherent, this is because the rules of American public activity borrow from other walks of life, whereas tradition in many European countries dictates the opposite pattern.

As we have seen, the game of American party politics allows substantial margins for adjustment, and this equilibrium can only be upset by the most exceptional circumstances. During the four decades that have followed World War II, this has only occurred three times, and each time it was touched off by a dramatic situation or emergency.

The first episode was the constellation of events known as "McCarthyism." During the toughest and most crucial stage of the cold war, a committee led by Senator Joseph McCarthy launched a vast campaign of allegations and intimidations to save a "pure" America from the danger of Communism and thus treason. All at once, the rules, practical compromises, bipartisan agreements on delicate issues, and cautious counterpositions of different viewpoints were shattered. Once the crisis was over, McCarthy's frenzied persecution and inquisition was dismissed as a fluke, because the two major parties and the Eisenhower administration had kept mainly out of it. Today, reexamination of the episode clearly shows that it was a case of role abuse, conducted by a minority with strong ideological motivations, in violation of, if not of specific rules, certainly of established traditions. The momentary popular success of McCarthy's movement was entirely due to its passionate manipulation of public opinion.

The second episode was not conceived in Congress. It began outside of Washington, its performers did not belong to the political ranks, and although it did possess some features common to mass movements, it influenced but was not able to change the political parties. This second phenomenon was the overwhelmingly black movement known in American history as the struggle for civil rights. In this case, two presidents—Kennedy and Johnson—did what Eisenhower had done during the previous "crisis": that is to say, they became moderators with the purpose of introducing America's institutions and political parties to a potentially revolutionary kind of ferment that had begun outside those institutions. In Eisenhower's case, the President had been forced at one point to oppose and stop the expanding aggression of Senator McCarthy's committee, because the tension caused by McCarthy was threatening to disrupt national harmony and equilibrium. Kennedy and Johnson felt it was their inevitable duty to convince the institutions to accept the civil rights movement, and they did this by supporting the movement's requests for new legislation. By forcing the institutions to favor the movement's demands, they assured themselves the consensus and clout necessary to defeat such sporadic offshoots of violence as the Black Panthers, the Black Muslims, black Marxism, and intellectual preaching about a "return to Africa."

So the second episode was unlike the first. Its political repercussions began as moral motivations and the political parties and institutions were involved at a later stage. Despite the nonnegotiable demands it made upon the nation's politicians, it was a nonparliamentary, nonpolitical movement of the masses. It began in the churches, not out of political collaboration. All of its leaders were pastors of black Protestant churches in the South, and they managed to create the first alliance of Catholic priests, Jewish rabbis, and Protestant ministers ever established in America. Finally, although the movement hoped to participate ultimately in dialogue with the parties and with federal government, it never meant to become a part of either one. Nor did it intend to direct decision making from within. Relying upon its strength as an external pressure group, it carefully built itself an incorruptible and strong image by remaining substantially detached from the political machine.

Later, as is well known, this clear-cut distinction was distorted by the countless adjustments and reassessments that enabled absorption of the aftershock. Aware of a hostile multitude and more sensitive to its troubles, the federal government tried to be as open as possible, and although the Nixon administration largely curtailed this trend, Carter restored it, and soon it was spreading from the White House to the judicial branch, civil service, and diplomacy. Meanwhile, the movement's respect for legality inspired its followers to believe in institutions and parties, so that relations began to be established with other nonpolitical but influential organizations, including some labor unions. Similarly, groups were mobilized to register the black population for the vote, because this was the only way to make sure the movement's demands would be met. In the end, Congressional participation increased, not dramatically, but enough to make a difference. Carter gave the movement Cabinet status by sending Andrew Young to the United Nations and Patricia Harris to the Department of Commerce.

There are many ways to explain the bonds that grew between the extraparliamentary masses of the civil rights battle and the Democratic Party: historically, they date from the New Deal era; others grew on the spot, thanks to the particular sensitivity of the Kennedy and Johnson camps. They did not necessarily result, as has frequently been surmised, from "natural and inevitable" relations between the movement and the party. After all, both civil rights presidents were supported by fiercely liberal Republicans and opposed by staunchly conservative Democrats. Of course, there is no denying the deep bond that has formed between the civil rights movement, or what is left of it, and the Democratic Party. Changes in American political equilibrium have not weakened this bond. But the Republican Party during the Reagan presidency has gradually redefined its position, moving away from its tradition of ignoring civil rights and rejecting the demands of the poor urban masses.

This is the setting for the third episode of special and unusual relations between the political system and pressure groups led by moral motivations. This time the movement is an aggregation of fundamentalist and evangelical groups. Once again the movement begins in the churches and not in the parties, because its demands are fueled by the frenzy of moral righteousness rather than by political strategy. Like the early civil rights movement, it too is in search of a political staging ground, and this time the Republican Party has welcomed the newcomers, in the wake of the psychological and organizational blows dealt by Vietnam and Watergate. But there are two important differences. This movement has been carefully orchestrated, and precise, direct techniques rule its relations with the host party. Rather than count upon a moral alliance or supply generic support, the Moral Majority and related groups make specific demands and well-defined offers. They ask for a radically conservative revision of almost every political program accepted in America today. In return they will provide a bureaucratic apparatus that includes everything from direct-mail campaigns to a proven ability to achieve specific goals. All this adds up to make the coalition a machine unmatched by anything ever seen in recent American politics.

Like the McCarthy committee and the civil rights movement, the Moral Majority is the protagonist of a crisis in America's domestic equilibrium. From the McCarthy experience, the moral majority seems to have inherited a tendency to attack rather than defend. And like the civil rights movement it draws upon wide popular support, the charismatic leadership of several nationally known personalities, a religious wellspring, and initial detachment from Congress and national institutions. It follows the same threefold strategy of invading political territory from a moral platform, superimposing its own church-inspired structure upon the organization of the parties, and coercing political groups into accepting demands that cannot be refused. Like the civil rights movement, it offers support and in exchange it requires solutions, in the form of new programs and court orders. And it relies upon one political party—Republican, in this case—to gain access to the institutions and thereby consolidate its influence upon them.

However, our analogy breaks down at this point, whence the Moral Majority swings in a direction the civil rights movement never took. Unlike its predecessor, the church coalition for which the Moral Majority speaks is not tempered by the heat of political contact, nor does it tread cautiously in the world of politics, for fear of destroying America's historical church-state separation. On the contrary, conflict makes this movement all the more intransigent, with the result that it virtually "occupies" and conditions its own political party. This is performed in part by sending an organized force of "missionaries" to infiltrate the party and Congress, and in part by showing clear signs of its power to eliminate enemies. In one swipe, it is able to "cleanse" the American public scene of such designated adversaries as Senators McGovern, Church, and Bayh and Congressman Brademas in the 1980 election. Here the Moral Majority makes its direction even clearer. The goals of the civil rights struggle were facts and problems, not individual grievances, and the leaders of the movement usually presented their demands with respect for traditional American tolerance in matters of cultural, historical, and institutional contrast. They allowed a wide margin for compromise, and only the decision to actively oppose the Vietnam War suddenly—and temporarily—hindered communications between the civil rights movement and a wide range of political "correspondents" in the Democratic Party. But the Moral Majority adopted a dual commitment to religion and politics from the very outset. It struck important public figures only because it considered their morality reprehensible, but in so doing it did not use the general criteria of Christian morality whence its inspiration derived but drew instead upon the canons and regulations of the most secular conservative ideology. Thus for the first time in American history, traditional separation between church and state has been dramatically bypassed.

THE NEW CHURCHES AND THE STATE

Which churches are behind the Moral Majority? Once again the analogy with the civil rights movement may help cast some light on the new vast conservative alliance. Both movements grew from the strategy of church aggregation that was germinated by Protestant fragmentation and the pastoral personality cult. Both were then cultivated in the fertile but mostly uncharted terrain of Baptist, fundamentalist, and evangelical congregations.

Two differences are immediately apparent. Whereas King's movement dealt cautiously with institutions in an attempt to maintain church-state separation, the new movement takes the demands of its faith straight to the state, heedless of this long-standing American tradition. Second, the Moral Majority has entirely different relations with the mainstream Council of Churches, which combines all the large Protestant denominations, with the Catholic Church, and with the organizations that represent the Jewish community and culture in America.

Here too the new Christian movement's feisty challenge has clearly distinguished it from previous political-religious movements. It has shrewdly delineated its strategy so that any issue extraneous to the coalition and its leadership can be ignored, be it on theological, charismatic, or religious grounds. But it has also had the presence of mind to center its programs around at least two points that were bound to attract the benevolent attention of other religious groups. By firmly and stubbornly opposing abortion, the neo-Christians gained the interest and then the support of the Catholic Church, and by declaring absolute and unquestioning support for Israel and its right to exist, they neatly circumvented ingrained Jewish suspicion regarding neo-Christian frenzy and thereby created yet another alliance.

However, the one important problem that still looms darkly over the fundamentalist evangelical movement is the skepticism with which the large Protestant churches and even such evangelical leaders as Billy Graham view their movement's cause. Indeed, the new coalition seems to have been founded more upon challenge than upon alliance. Wherever it seems impossible or unwise to reach an agreement, its strategy is to attack. Relations with the older evangelical churches are ambiguous and rarely exceed an exchange of letters or limited mutual acknowledgement, which does little to camouflage the existing climate of competition. As for relations with the large Protestant denominations, both sides began on an antagonistic foot. On the one hand, the neo-Christians immediately condemned mainstream American Protestantism, and they were met with diffidence from churches whose longstanding tradition of tolerance and liberalism has always led them to establish a clear distinction between political and religious affairs. Of course this diffidence was also an expression of fears that the new churches might profit from the Protestant tradition of fragmentation, exodus, and passage from one church to another. Indeed, statistics show that the neo-Christian groups have been enjoying a significant increase in membership, but no such trend has been seen in the mainstream Protestant churches. But the movement's growth is certainly not related only to individual choice.

A plethora of smaller churches and sects cannot help being attracted to the new coalition, above all because of their analogous social and geographical background. All these groups draw upon a middle or lower-middle class population living in vast agrarian and provincial regions of the country, particularly in the south and the southwest, where local culture is far removed from the large cities that are considered to be breeding grounds of liberalism and sin. Mythification of the past supplies natural compensation for the alienation and threat posed by this isolation from the cities and large universities. The patriotism that accompanies these values seems to express a need to reaffirm bonds between the small provincial town and the whole country, although this has been overlooked by the parties and ignored by the media.

The inbred hostility to news and mass media comes from a sense of cultural inequality and a feeling that the provincial image and culture have been ignored, if not denigrated. Finally, the typically Protestant tendency toward continual fragmentation has led many congregations to adopt theologically modest and intellectually impoverished platforms that have made them even further marginal. In these circumstances, the neo-Christian coalition seems to be a good protective umbrella. By huddling together under one umbrella, these tiny sects acquire— or feel they have acquired—national acknowledgement and a right to reject the culture of big cities, official churches, and large cultural centers.

The small churches have gained this widescale status thanks to their active and intelligent use of the media. Analysis of local religious radio and television stations in America would show that by merely switching from private to electronic preaching religious groups can create a sense of social promotion. This may even be translated into a theological verification of possession of the truth. The use of television by small churches and sects has grown to gigantic proportions, so that isolated subcultures can reach an astounding number of people through Christian TV networks capable of covering multistate areas and the exchange programs that exist between different networks.

CATHOLICS, JEWS, AND CHRISTIAN FUNDAMENTALISM

Relations with Catholicism are still ambiguous and troublesome. Whereas the Catholic Church greatly appreciates and supports the neo-Christian antiabortion campaign, it is uneasy with and even hostile to the movement's neoconservative preaching. This ambivalence exposes it to the risk of losing its followers to neo-Christian recruitment. Fundamentalist relations with American Jewish culture and tradition are at least equally if not more rocky, because of the new Christians' willful swing from the religious to the secular and from theology to politics.

Christian fundamentalism has never been affected by the self-examination to which the Catholic Church (with the Second Vatican Council) and the mainstream Protestant churches have put themselves in their attempts to rid themselves of any religious or cultural consequences of racial discrimination. Indeed, during the massive neo-evangelical National Affairs Briefing held in Dallas in August 1980, it was publically stated that "God Almighty does not hear the prayer of a Jew." Clearly, this statement touched off an immediate wave of scandal and astonishment throughout America.

Yet most of the churches and cults which attended that immense meeting, whose tens of thousands of participants were mostly ministers and pastors of innumerable tiny churches scattered throughout the country, had already sworn allegiance to the Moral Majority's founding principles, including the most loudly proclaimed of them all, support at any cost for "the present boundaries" of Israel and even for the affirmation of "Zionism." This objective—support for Israel—seemed to openly contradict the movement's primary goal of establishing the purity of Christianity, and the inevitable result was considerable discomfort on the part of America's Jewish community, which suddenly found itself caught halfway between appreciation and disapproval. As early as November 18, 1980, only a few days after Ronald Reagan's election and the victory of conservatism, which many American Jews enthusiastically welcomed, the American Jewish Committee published a trend analysis officially dedicated to the New Right but almost entirely focused upon the neo-Christian movement and its contradictory attitudes toward Jewish culture.

The report favorably acknowledges the new Christian movement's declared passionate support for Israel, logically placing it within an overall conservative point of view dedicated to maintaining international balance and containing any threat of Communism, the inevitable consequence of which is intransigent defense of the status quo in Israel. Naturally, it was not the study's purpose to discover other reasons fot this spontaneous declaration of "Zionism," but if its authors had looked they might have found a desire to challenge the United Nations and its famous resolution number 242, which requires that Israel return the territories it now occupies. Still, this was not a stand on international politics. It was more likely an expression of hostility toward such "cosmopolitan, sinful, and morally unreliable" institutions as the United Nations. In addition, it was a good way to establish bonds with the American Jewish community and thereby head off any suspicion that would naturally be aroused by a Christian movement so culturally remote and historically alien to American and world Judaism. And indeed, the American Jewish Committee's assessment of the cultural and historical nature of the neo-Christian movement behind the New Right did reveal caution bordering upon mistrust.

Rabbi Arthur Hertzberg, vice-president of the World Jewish Congress, observed:

These movements are inevitably inclined toward discrimination, because they call for absolute faith in a very few principles. One of these principles is redemption in Christ. Here, however, the theologically tolerant ecumenical vision of modern Christianity has been replaced by the rigid intolerance that is the natural heritage of cultural isolation. Instead of a clearly defined body of theological material, a handful of principles is repeated *ad infinitum;* furthermore, these are said to be absolutes and as such are exempt from cultural analogy or theological confrontation. With the exception of total support for Israel, all religious positions of the neo-Christian groups contain implicit and unconscious elements of discrimination; they are the expression of a tiny culture incapable of understanding, accepting, or tolerating other cultures. Some years ago there was a move to publish a Christian Yellow Pages, which would have enabled church followers to establish exclusive business relations with other believers. The discriminatory consequences of such a publication would have been enormous."

Rabbi Hertzberg's diffidence should be regarded less in the light of his liberal position close to the Democratic Party than as an expression—perhaps more loudly voiced than others—of the unease destined to remain widespread throughout the Jewish community with regard to the new Christians, despite the latter group's proposed allegiance on the issue of support for Israel. Indeed, even Reverend Falwell's use of the term "Zionism" is regarded with skepticism, if not outright disblief, by many Jewish leaders.

The infamous Dallas statement regarding God's supposed deafness to Jewish prayers was followed by an avalanche of justifications, apologies, and rectifications. But despite the Moral Majority's attempts to right the wrong done, most Jewish leaders have maintained an attitude of caution and cool detachment. A meeting between the two groups was held in New York at the end of January 1981, but the committee later refused to participate in the formulation of a joint statement, and the neoevangelical representative was only able to tell television reporters, "We have taken note of our respective theological positions."

THE MANIFESTO OF FUNDAMENTALIST CHRISTIANITY

It has already been said that the great historical and political interest attached to the story of religion in America is justified by the basic relation that exists between religious persuasion and social behavior. If problems related to the new fundamentalist and evangelical fervor now serve as a standard by which to measure all the other positions, it is not because the movement is of particular cultural or theological import, but because it seems to stand for facts, positions, and militancies that explain and anticipate current political events. The best way to explore this is to define the code words of new activism, inasmuch as they define the movement's strategy with regard to other cultures and groups, and in relation to the political parties and institutions. But beyond this examination, which really amounts to the description of actual and eventual conflicts in contemporary America, there are several underlying questions. Why has the neo-Christian revival taken the form of a classic right-wing movement so rigidly oriented to the past? Is it history's compensation for the supposed leftward swing of the other religious movement for civil rights, or are the tensions voiced by the coalition so overwhelming that they could only surface outside the parties and institutions? And why is there so much clout behind the demand for a conservative and Christian reorganization of the American way of life and of America's relations with the world?

One example might be as follows. The large Protestant churches which formed centuries ago and have now totally penetrated the establishment have tended over the years to accept novelties, reforms, and social visions and conceptions that took advantage of church tolerance to replace the "religious" with the "nonreligious." Because they were bound to govern together, the churches and the political institutions grew accustomed to collaborating and adapting to fulfill bureaucratic, social, and economic necessities. So liberal democracy became a culture in which religion and its attendant institutions played a part in every facet of public and social life. There has never been a church-state conflict in all the history of the United States, nor has any church ever exercised the kind of temporal authority that ruled Europe for centuries.

Simultaneously, liberal democracy has undergone sweeping change in order to coexist with industrial development and its need for mobility, freedom from prejudice, and rigorous evaluation of personal and professional worth. The cultural history of America, as well as relations between science, culture, and social organization on the one hand and religion on the other, have been upset by a succession of abrupt leaps backward and marked by clamorous bounds forward. In this century, there have been two outstanding backward leaps. The first was prohibition, the frenzy for moral purity that sprang from a combination of fundamentalist nostalgia and a yearning for perfection that was drawn from literal interpretation of the Divine Word. The second episode was the celebrated Scopes trial, in which a teacher stood accused of having introduced Darwin's evolution theory to students in an American school.

The very nation that so proudly hailed itself as the home of the free and the exporter of tolerance—in the name of which it had already fought World War I and would soon unleash all of its cultural, moral, and military might upon Nazism—had now run aground amid problems that undoubtedly seemed irrelevant and ridiculous to the rest of the world opinion. Even the long and painful experience of racism, which continued illegally but widely throughout a thriving industrial society, until it was spotlighted by the civil rights "revolt," was often motivated by thinly disguised religious fervor. It is interesting to note that America has never had an antiblack or racist political movement based upon secular principles or dictates, with the exception of minuscule Nazi groups. Motivation for racist behavior has always been attributed to the Bible, and even the least religious of all racist movements, the Ku Klux Klan, uses the cross for its symbol.

However, liberal and progressive causes have undergone the same trends. A comparison between the two types of episode, with backward leaps and forward bounds always caused by religious fervor, testifies to the essential features of American culture, in which moral inspiration has outweighed all other factors since the country's founding and all through its historical development. But such a comparison also explains how the call for purity of the religious principle has always influenced the leaders of religious factions to avoid seeking more than marginal political allegiance or support and to withold it themselves except under brief and limited circumstances. The courts, not Congress, have been the battleground for morality-motivated clashes between opposing camps. It was a court that debated the problem of Darwinism. And before Presidents Kennedy and Johnson convinced Congress to intervene with new legislation, a multitude of courts had already begun supporting the cause of civil rights.

The description of America's religiously motivated social controversy and ferment shows how different the country's pastoral and ecclesiastical traditions have been in the past, when compared, for example, with those of Ireland, where such Protestant personalities as Ian Paisley and such Catholic leaders as Bernadette Devlin have made certain that political controversy contained decidely religious overtones. But now the same sort of attitude has appeared in America, as a result of the new alliance between fundamentalist Christians and conservative Republicans.

The relevance of this new backward leap is demonstrated by the long list of code words that represent the neo-Christian position. On the one hand the neo-Christian movements mobilize to oppose the mainstream Protestant churches because they feel they have surrendered too much of Christian teaching and integrity to the demands of coexisting harmoniously with the state and the social structure. On the other hand, they are alarmed by the unrest, disorder, and tension created by antiwar movements and crises like Watergate. Overall is a climate of seeming permissiveness that is intolerable to fundamentalists.

It never occurred to the neo-Christian movement that it might be possible to revitalize the church from within, because theirs is an unreconcilable challenge to the mainstream church's pact of tolerance with the nation's culture and institutions. This culture originates in the big cities and large universities, and so it is hostile, undesirable, and alien. The neo-Christians' obvious plan has been to give their anti-establishment movement clear political overtones in order to produce a socially explosive mixture of forces reminiscent of—albeit opposite to—the Vietnam movement and the cultural halo which encircled it during the sixties.

One case in point is seen in relations between the New Christian Right and evangelical preaching once conducted by such celebrities as Billy Graham. Although he came from the same culturally ephemeral ranks of evangelicalism, the fundamentalists saw Graham's church as a mainstream congregation. Thus the confines of new evangelicalism have eliminated not only Catholic bishops and Protestant ministers but even its own famous leaders, regardless of their popularity with enormous audiences. The reason is straightforward: Graham has shown himself to be a moderate, whereas the new movement aims for intransigence. Moreover, there is the aspect of heedless invasion of the political field. The secular fracture of the sixties left the new religious movement with the feeling that the only place it could regain the ground it had lost was outside the churches and inside the parties. Because one of these parties was "weak and empty"—Hubert Humphrey's expression was clearly a partisan opinion, yet it was not entirely unfounded, considering the long period of post-Nixon crisis—the movement found itself face-to-face with an inviting opportunity.

Were these conditions enough to activate the strongly conservative tendencies of the new coalition and affect its way of conducting politics, which was to eliminate progressive members of Congress and replace them with passionate and forceful representatives of the new morality? Is this sufficient explanation of what at the onset of the eighties appears to be the strongest and most effective alliance based on principles and organization ever established in America between a church coalition and a political organization? There is no question that we are dealing with a unique episode: for the first time a "church," this one embracing all the groups that make up the Moral Majority and the vast conglomeration of neo-evangelicals, has marched directly onto the political field to propose its men, programs, threats, laws, and visions.

RELIGIOUS REVOLUTION OF THE MIDDLE-CLASS

There is one solid economic argument that may explain the force of these two trends, the first based upon religious frenzy and the second upon aggressive political activism. The accomplishments of the American dream have created an enormous middle class, proud of its climb out of poverty but irritated by its inability to celebrate its "harvest" in the carefree manner it feels it has earned. The political establishment that has governed almost uninterruptedly since Roosevelt's time continues to formulate collective goals, community duties, and responsibilities for other groups' needs. Taxes are a burden, prosperity gradually erodes, those who have been left out increase their demands. Then there are the troubles of the school system, with middle-class children forcedly bused to poorer neighborhoods so the nation can achieve its goal of integrated schooling; housing; inflation; and increasingly widespread humiliation as a result of international blunders. The Protestant or "Protestantized" middle class has paid the price for the continual pragmatic compromises that successive governments have had to impose in order to maintain internal peace and international coexistence in the face of change, newly emerging forces, new challenges, and new dangers

Why is it that some portions of the American middle class are overburdened by government and not, as occurs in Europe and Latin America, "provoked by the affluence of the privileged classes"? Once again, the answer lies in the Protestant culture, with its emphasis not on the group but on each individual and the degree of practical and moral self-affirmation and achievement he has attained. Intellectuals in government, with their abstract explanations of the world, their tendency to consider too many differing reasons and interests, their propensity to look for the "general" aspect of the problem, and their obsession with the apparently mysterious nature of economic facts and international events, are irritating, alien, and unbearable.

Thus this public, which is obviously larger than politicians had calculated and less pliable than the liberal media had presumed, has been motivated by economic tribulations and its own long-felt but unexpressed repugnance for the complications of domestic and international politics; and by a relentless search for uncompromising integrity upon which to base its authentic revolt. The movement found passionate spokesmen in the right wing of the Republican Party, which in turn has been "renewed" by the religious component, whose fervor far exceeds the secular conservatism of Barry Goldwater. This political trend has probably just begun to surface, and it is very likely that we have only seen the beginning of the moral and religious demands on the basis of which this faction intends to exert its influence and eventually influence the government.

Thus a variety of interlocking reasons explain the political and moral, individual and public issues being expressed at this particular moment in history, in the name of nonnegotiable values. The inherent nonnegotiability of neo-Christian moral values is a reason in itself for conservative political behavior. Religious movements currently enjoying political prominence came from areas that have been overlooked during the last fifty years of cultural evolution in the nation. It is possible that the secular wing of American neo-conservatism, including the President, some of his Cabinet members, counselors and collaborators, and the conservative members of Congress elected in 1980, plans to give the fundamentalist movement more space in exchange for its acceptance to a degree of compromise and its acknowledgement of the natural need for political moderation. If this has been the intention, the present decade may prove it to be a bit of a gamble. The proof, or probability, that the movement has no intention to compromise, at least in the short run, lies in the code words that stand for neo-Christianity's demands upon national and international policy.

CODE WORDS OF THE NEW CHRISTIAN RIGHT

The first code word used by the new coalition is no newcomer to American culture; its contemporary use, however, is unique. Today, when new Christians speak of "human rights," they are referring above all to the absolute and nonnegotiable prohibition of abortion. The movement has demanded that Congress reform the Constitution by adding what it has called the Human Rights Amendment, on the basis of which abortion would be inadmissible and thus considered murder, no matter what the circumstances. This is tantamount to imposing official Christian morality upon a secular state.

And yet the strategic use of this code word must be appreciated, for with it fundamentalism has captured the same spirit of morality crusade given to the issue by the head of the Catholic Church. For the first time, the nonnegotiability of abortion, so staunchly defended by Pope John Paul II, has created an axis of agreement between fundamentalist Protestantism and the very core of Catholicism. Moreover, the unprecedented emotional drive behind this convergence seems capable of mobilizing Catholics on another issue traditionally kept in the dark and now revived as a sort of twin issue by the new alliance: the death penalty. Theologically, contemporary Catholicism shares nothing with the New Christian Right on this point. But once it has been enlisted in the antiabortion crusade, Catholic leaders might have a tough time ordering their flock to ignore the equally peremptory demands for a return to capital punishment.

The same impulse has contaminated American Jewish opinion, even among urban populations which are usually the most inclined to practice tolerance. Here the alliance has wielded its might in the opposite direction. Whereas its biblical and cultural traditions make it less adverse to the death penalty, Jewish culture should have every reason to resist the antiabortion drive, given the movement's clearly Christian revivalist overtones. But just as the code word "abortion" has enticed the Catholics to support the death penalty with a militancy heretofore unknown, so the Jewish community may be willing to adopt a new and unnatural intransigence on the issue of abortion in exchange for a more widespread inclination to accept capital punishment.

The New Christian Right's code words have readily been accepted by many political figures who realize they can no longer ignore the clout and impact of such a coalition. Then there are the unvoiced but easily perceivable social, economic, and political motivations behind the movement's success: with cities in crisis and criminality paralyzing the middle class, the result has been a call to extend the definitions of crime in order to inflict stronger punishment. The cries for the death penalty express a basic need for liberation, in which the penalty has all the force of a crusade and "just punishment" staves off fear.

All of these motivations make it impossible to show the new Christians how incoherent it is to fight for life against abortion on the one hand and call for death to punish transgression on the other. The peremptory nature of the two associated demands overrules any debate.

THE DREAM OF THE CITADEL

Another code word is "family morality," the implications of which extend to numerous areas and require strict reform, part of which seems aimed at official segregation or at least de facto separation of the races. One example are the thousands of "Christian schools" born in the name of protecting family morality. These segregated white institutions subtract a vast number of children from public schools which are integrated by law and, thanks to years of struggle, by habit. Undoubtedly, neo-Christian strategy has taken account of the anxiety, uncertainty, and confusion that exist not only among its own ranks, but also in groups that would otherwise have no particular reason to "convert." In many areas American public schools have badly deteriorated. The dangers of drugs and violence and the relegation of one's children to an alien culture are countered by a seemingly reassuring, disciplined, and pure world where the neo-Christian dream of returning to the past can come true. While there may be many a family for whom the fundamentalist Christian teaching practiced in these private schools means little, those same families greatly appreciate the supervision and safe conditions their children will find there. The image of a tiny fortress in a devastated countryside laid waste by the ravages of war is a very successful one indeed, and it has broadened the base of support for fundamentalism.

It is this search for safety and guaranteed security, something federal and local governments seem unable to provide, and not a return to racism, that has really made "Christian schools" successful. It would be hard to say if this is yet another strategic intuition on the part of the new churches of the right. Certainly, they have a sincere calling, which is to disseminate the "gospel." And most families who send their children to the new schools are motivated by something very much like what prompted Italian farmers, who were anything but religious, to send their own sons to seminaries rather than to public schools at the turn of the century.

However, the code word "family morality" stands for manifold local and national strategies and these requests, demands, and testimonies have fanned out to flood into many aspects of public life with their nonnegotiable calls for reform. The first to feel this effect has been television, fiercely accused of serving as a vehicle for immorality. The anti-television crusade was launched along with the war on pornography, and here again remarkable organizational instinct has seen to it that highly diversified militants and masses join forces. For instance, there are the "feminists against pornography," whose aim is to protect the image of woman from the abuse to which the porn industry has usually subjected it; there are the antiporn merchants, who feel threatened by unrespectable competition that has no place in their communities; there are naturally concerned parents whose children are exposed to the violence often accompanying pornography; there are charitable Catholic groups, who focus their battle against this social blight upon the redemption of its victims.

None of these and other groups involved had ever thought of organizing a united front for censorship, but that is exactly what the New Right has proposed with its blacklist of television programs. The boycott works by dissuading sponsors from buying commercial time on the blacklisted shows. American commercial television is supported entirely by public response, so that such a threat must be weighed most seriously. The companies that advertise on the networks pay significant sums in exchange for prestigious exposure, and they cannot possibly risk turning that prestige into disgrace by ignoring the undesirable program hit list.

The movement's code words indicate tendencies, not achievements, and their success is still uncertain. However, there is no doubt about the efficiency of the fundamentalist and conservative Christian organization. When one thinks of the size and enormity of this country and the limitations and restrictions of the decision-making group in the popular entertainment business, it is not hard to imagine the alienation and hostile antagonism existing among those who for whatever reason feel they are the objects and not the subjects of television production. Thus once again it seems that the neo-Christian groups have established an effective relationship between moral objectives, political mobilization, and operational strategies. With its powerful drive, the coalition can unite psychological, cultural, and historical motivations which for years have provoked fear, isolation, and discontent. Above all, it has promised to achieve simple goals, enforce strict behavioral rules, and protect its flock within the walls of the Christian citadel.

While it is true that the new coalition will surely benefit from this sturdy chain of fresh allegiances, it is doubtful that it will ever wish to collaborate in drawing up its manifestoes for faith and morality. Neo-Christianity has nothing to negotiate with anyone. The forcefulness of its leadership, unprecedented in all the history of world Protestantism, is at stake here. For instance, among the implications and consequences of the code word "family morality" are demands for mandatory school prayer, an unflinching campaign to get homosexuals out of every form of public activity, and the battle to defeat ERA, the Equal Rights Amendment designed to give women irreversible judicial parity based upon the Constitution.

Clearly, by sticking to these three campaigns the movement risks jeopardizing its relations with other religions, first by forcing Christian prayers upon children who live in a pluralistic country, and then by upsetting its own delicate balance within the political and cultural fabric of the nation. And yet much will depend upon the coalition's momentum as it constantly offers one issue in exchange for another: support for Israel in exchange for the Christianization of the country; consolidation of the anti-abortion forces in exchange for other deep-felt Catholic values; support for a conservative economic program in exchange for the moralistic boycott of "anti-Christian" television programs, which are almost always inspired by liberalism and tolerance.

THE "UNITE AND DIVIDE" STRAGEGY

Over the past few years, state and city governments in many areas of America have been besieged by neo-Christian demands for legislative proposals such as the "sequeal rule" adopted by the Department of Health and Human Services and published in the *Federal Register*, January 25, 1983. It provides for immediate involvement of parents at any time a minor calls for medical assistance related to sexual activity from birth control devices to treatment of venereal disease. Strong pressure generated by neo-religious groups over conservative legislators, with White House support, has created heated debates that involve the basic issue of civil liberties and the practical problem of assisting minors in trouble.

This reveals another unique feature of neo-Christian fundamentalism: its simple issues and universal themes appear to create unity, but that surface harmony is actually stretched tightly across a framework of tensions that reflect only fundamentalist thought and its conception of morality. Granted, this vision lends itself nicely to the construction of alliances; indeed, the exaltation of the past (the role of family and parental authority) is really a cry for more solid and more secure social organization. But the fundamentalist outlook is also just as capable of generating conflict, even within the conservative pact it has established with the post-1980 reincarnation of the Republican Party.

Another initiative which has caused considerable discomfort among Catholics, Jews, and the Protestant Council of Churches is the blacklist of books destined for school libraries. The limits set by this list are a far cry from traditional American tolerance. What is more, they not only challenge or oppose groups that have already established other ties with the neo-Christians (i.e., the Catholics and the Jews) but they even defy secular neoconservatism. One blacklist presented at the beginning of 1981 quickly became the object of passionate debate and confused disciplinary and judicial action. The blacklist was first made public by an AP dispatch on July 1, 1981. On February 7, 1982, Kurt Vonnegut wrote an open letter to the *New York Times* about the censorship of his books. On May 9, 1982. the *Times* carried a full-page appeal against the "Christian Blacklist of Books" sponsored by an ad hoc committee against censorship called "People for the American Way." The list named such works as

The Fixer, by Bernard Malamud, *Slaughterhouse Five*, by Kurt Vonnegut, *Soul on Ice*, by Eldridge Cleaver, *The Naked Ape*, by Desmond Morris, *The Best Short Stories by Negro Writers*, edited by Langston Hughes, and *Black Boy*, by Richard Wright.

The list stands out because of the many ways it can be read. Malamud may have been ostracized because of the "scandalous" theme of his banned short story, or perhaps because he is among the foremost spokesmen for American Jewish traditions and life-styles. It may have been the fierce pacifism of Vonnegut's book that got him blacklisted, or it might have been his disbelief in the "righteousness" of World War II, or his brutal description of several war scenes. On the other hand, Vonnegut's "downfall" may have been the language that made him famous, for it is an aggressive and uninhibited mode of speech that certainly does not conform to the religious sensitivity of the neo-Christians. *The Naked Ape* is clearly condemned for its links with evolution theory, which the fundamentalists so adamantly reject. Many of the other censored authors are blacks, and here again there may be different reasons, either the latent racism mentioned earlier, or the occasional brutality of some of their texts. Perhaps all of these motivations are inherent in the whole project, which is to reject anything that is alien, be it because of language, nature, or values. Things of this sort have been occurring for several years now in the United States, but the tendency seems to have picked up steam, at the same time that passion behind the allegations has grown while protest and resistance have dwindled.

One code word that certainly lies at the very core of neo-fundamentalist Christian strategy is "creationism." Requests to exclude the teaching of evolution theory from public schools have deluged dozens of local courts and legislatures. Many teachers have responded with resistance, and this has been one of the causes for the spread of the private Christian schools. Even so, resistance has not stemmed the flow of indictments and trials. Wherever public opinion has been least willing to give in, neo-Christians have clung to their demands for equal time: if a

teacher mentions Darwin, he or she must also quote the Bible
and explain its interpretation. Everywhere, the fundamentalists seem to have drawn encouragement from the silence of most
local and national politicians unwilling to involve themselves in
debate. Even in televised round table discussions, Darwin is
usually defended by an enraged educator because, apparently,
no senator or congressman is eager to take sides on this matter.

Headquarters for the anti-Darwin crusade are at the Creation Science Research Center in San Diego. The center's director, Robert Kofahl, acquired his good credentials at the California Institute of Technology. However, Kofahl specialized in
chemistry, not biology, anthropology, or other sciences that
would have justified his self-appointed title of "creationist scientist." Not one member of America's cultural or scientific establishment has joined the center or Kofahl or the creationist
cause. Yet it would be wrong to consider this a losing or isolated battle. The Creation Science Research Center is one of
the outposts in a far-flung army of centers set up by neo-Christian coalition. As such, it receives substantial funding, it is able
to inundate the media with material, and it has access to
hundreds of television and radio stations that belong either directly or indirectly to the movement. Moreover, as we have seen,
it benefits from the unwillingness of the most visible public figures, particularly politicians, to take a stand on the issue.

Behind the San Diego center stands a broad range of institutions, including the Bible Science Association in Minneapo-
lis; the Geo-Science Research Institute run by the Seventh-Day
Adventist Church in Loma Linda, California; the Creation Research Quarterly in Ann Arbor; and dozens of groups that have
carefully included the word "science" in their title, established
their offices in large university towns such as Ann Arbor and
Berkeley, and even used the university's name to give the public and the media the impression that they have working relations with legitimate centers for scientific research.

The creationist attack strategy is a model for operations that
may one day increase dramatically to cover broader public, cul-

tural, and political territory. The first element in this strategy is preliminary formation of the ranks. Young fundamentalist church members are encouraged to attend the best universities, where they can study under well-known scientists. When they appear to have sufficient credentials, they abandon university research to join the creationist camp, finding employment in its research centers or at the publishing houses that print and distribute the centers' material. By scrupulously publicizing their scientific credentials, these people lend technical credibility to the theological interpretation they propose.

The second strategic element is "negativism." The creationists like to begin debate in the scientific arena, concentrating their resources on the search for possible incongruities, errors, or gaps in the Darwinian position. Only after they have demonstrated that evolutionism can be disputed do they refer to the Bible's creationist vision of a world literally created in seven days, citing the inevitable proof of its accuracy. "If Darwin is wrong, then the scientific truth *must* lie in the Bible."

What kind of impact have the creationist groups had on American public opinion? News or statistical surveys would seem to indicate that it has been modest. But let us not forget the reticence of politicians to involve themselves in this controversy, a factor that is further accentuated by two others. First, although the creationists have sought to accredit themselves in the world of higher education, they have directed the main force of their battle toward the elementary and secondary schools. Second, the simple, fundamental issues of creationism are attractive, especially at a time when "complications"—in economic as well as foreign affairs—are considered by most people to be the very source of all evil.

This desire for simplification is what makes it relatively easy for fundamentalists to offer themselves as allies to superconservative politics. It may also be the reason that dramatic contradictions among differing neo-Christian positions and articles of faith have been overlooked by much of public opinion and the new political establishment. On the contrary, often these con-

tradictions seem to work in the new groups' favor. For instance, the Catholic Church has not seemed to notice that the
unified anti-abortion front has shifted Catholics toward other
positions that they might not actually share, whether for political, cultural, or historical reasons, or even because of Church
dogma itself. For one thing, there is the fundamentalist tendency to equate abortion with murder, combined with an equally
passionate demand that murder and every other serious offence
be punished by death.

The Jewish community has been so enthusiastic about the
secular and religious fundamentalist support of Israel that it now
seems willing to overlook the neo-Christian demand for a "pure"
Christianized America, which not only conflicts with traditional
Jewish liberalism but has always served as a historical cause and
framework for discrimination. Sooner or later, neo-Christian
fervor will demand a head count of Christians and non-Christians, and this has always caused incidents of anti-Semitism in
the past. Of course, such outbreaks have always been promptly
denied by one side and deliberately ignored by the other, but
they are still a source of friction.

THE VITALITY OF THE NEW CHURCHES

There are historical and cultural circumstances that have helped
Christian fundamentalist groups to come together and develop.
There is the inevitable conservatism of an intransigent vision
unwilling to mutate in accordance with history; likewise, there
is the unavoidable connection with conservative politics, be it
merely strategic or mutually convenient. Whatever the case, the
new movement's strength would suggest that the popularity of
religious conservatism is no happenstance or momentary fad.

Religious conservatism sets rigid limits based on its nonnegotiable outlook and "natural" and historical tendency to hold
an inflexible view of reality. As a result, the alliance that has
formed between religious and secular worlds should tend to
possess similar authoritarian features. We have seen that one

component in this new alliance is the desire for simplification. Because simplification is based upon absolutes, it requires unquestioning faith in a well-defined, limited set of values. The return to the past is also successful, inasmuch as whatever is over and done with is familiar and can be appreciated, and almost always seems better than present reality. So simplification has always been a strategic expedient of conservative politics.

A second component is the element of discipline: clear-cut situations imply simple choices and disciplined execution of those choices. From this come the dual requests for capital punishment and international intransigency. A third component is hostility toward the kinds of adventures and tolerance that attract liberal culture. This extends to all public welfare institutions, women's rights, gay rights, and the United Nations, and it testifies to a general dislike of anything "different." Because this distaste is not clearly expressed in terms of either religion or politics, it appears to indicate a general tendency toward discrimination. The demand for the death penalty puts an end to any typically "liberal" dispute over the fairness of retribution for crime.

There is also uncertainty and annoyance with poverty, which Christian fundamentalism usually considers to be what the poor have brought upon themselves with their own lack of righteousness. There is anger with the request to be indulgent with anyone, be he sinner or criminal or rebel or underprivileged, be it in public or private life. Religious fundamentalism has greatly helped political conservatism by eliminating the cumbersome values of *pietas* and compassion. The fundamentalists believe in "retribution with no exceptions," as manifested in absolute faith and little or no interest in charity. This makes it possible for conservative political strategy to ruthlessly mold its programs with no concern for personal, private, or abnormal situations, including poverty and the great Christian extenuation of charity. It also justifies rejection of what President Carter intended when he referred to "human rights."

Thus from two different sources comes public authorization

which had been discontinued: it is now admissible to be and declare oneself to be a bigot. Because this bigotry is cut off from its past by several decades of authentic social revolution that had effectively outlawed it, it may now seem to be surprisingly fresh and intriguingly courageous. The connotations of this new bigotry are mutable and adaptable; there is certainly no adequate correspondance between its intensity in the religious camp and the occasional, even opportunistic, way it is used in politics.

There were no racist motivations behind the Reagan administration's austerity program to sharply reduce a budget blown badly out of proportion by slipshod management. But if such intentions had existed, the fundamentalists would not have obstructed them. Likewise, there was no anti-Catholic intent in the administration's policy in Central America, even though it did oppose most Latin American bishops. This was a case of strategy, however disputable. At any rate, if neo-Christian support had been required, it would have been forthcoming.

In general, bigotry generates discrimination, and it raises several questions. Will political power be strong enough to resist contamination if it is ever forced to rally this support? Or will intransigent fundamentalists give up their passionate and nonnegotiable demands without a fight when events make it necessary for politicians to choose other forms of equilibrium and pragmatic collaboration? Political conservatism has shown that it is indebted to the neofundamentalist masses that support it. How and when will it pay this debt without identifying itself with those nonnegotiable values?

THE CONFLICT ABOUT FAITH AND CHARITY

My analysis of Christian fundamentalism has emphasized the reasons for its wide appeal to both religious and nonreligious audiences; for its ability to penetrate areas not usually reached by preaching; for the natural and strategically created common issues that have enabled construction of a network of support systems, exchange programs, and alliances. My intention has been to demonstrate the strength, as well as the capacity for duration and expansion, of a phenomenon that first appeared on the American scene at the end of the sixties.

On the other hand, there is the controversial side of the neo-Christian movement. As its demands grow, it may begin to clash with the needs and goals of political and secular conservatism. But as the movement's designs are perfected and clarified, they are also bound to erupt into possibly vicious conflict with the mainstream churches.

One element of contradiction that is clearly destined to grow exists now within the Catholic Church. The social culture promoted by Catholicism is already on a potential collision course with fundamentalism over the issues of charity and aid to the poor. The neo-Christians have never participated in any form of social action designed to help, to assist, and to comfort the disadvantaged. But as social problems of the poor increase, partly due to neoconservative reorganization of the economy and production, the Catholic church will find itself increasingly called upon to aid the needy. Where social and poltical conditions are constantly exposed to mass communication, this charitable attitude cannot be concealed, and this will result in greater verbal and political militancy.

The historical development and inner equilibrium of Catholicism make it unlikely that the Church will ever wholeheartedly embrace conservatism. The international nature of the religion would make it impossible, and the internal history of the American Catholic church indicates that such a change is highly improbable. It is difficult to say if hard-line confrontation between Catholicism and conservatism will take place over doctrine or social policy, but it would be unwise to assume that no issue will ever cause conflict or incompatibility between the Catholic hierarchy and the new fundamentalists. On February 16, 1984, the Reverend James Swaggart stated on a pre-recorded program broadcast by Channel 13 in New York that "All the work of Mother Thereas—and I repeat, all the charity work she has done in her life—means nothing. Absolutely nothing in terms of her salvation."

The international aspect is even more delicate. The world interests and culture of the Catholic Church always force it to oppose any government's dream of hegemony, even though this opposition may only materialize in the form of cautious hints and delicate strategies. This is partly due to Catholicism's instinctive alienation from any power but its own, even if that power is today strictly limited to spiritual matters. It also comes from actual need: too many Catholics are exposed to aggression and conflict, in many areas of the world and they cannot be abandoned by the Church. The problems posed for American Catholicism by Central America and the Philippines have never applied in the cases of Iran or the Middle East. One cannot expect the Catholic Church and its American bishops to be silent on the fate of Catholic countries.

The death penalty issue has caused some of the most delicate conflicts within cultures and positions in the last few decades. Because Catholics are part of the huge middle class that has been frightened by a loss of its rights, by the burden of too many responsibilities, and by the constant risk of crime, the Church cannot ignore massive cries for capital punishment. But it was only a few years ago that a Catholic mayoral candidate in New York City, Mario Cuomo, lost because he opposed the death penalty, while Governor Cary, another Catholic, continued to the end to veto a law approved twice by the New York State Assembly. Thus even the ethnic majorities in the Catholic Church have resisted neofundamentalist demands, and this is one more reason to imagine that Catholicism will continue to raise its formidable weapons in strong opposition to the new wave of conservatism it already mistrusts on both theological and historical grounds. In this area, there seems to be an unbreakable bond between the Catholics and the National Council of Churches, which represents most Protestant denominations. Thanks to neo-Christian zeal, there is already a solid wall of profound irritation surrounding all these mainstream churches.

Over the years, the profile of the American Catholic Church has been affected and changed by mainline Protestantism, but one may say, the Council of Churches has also been affected by the Catholic model of social action, and there have been frequent instances of practical cooperation and alliance between the two.

At this point we should consider once again the connection with Jewish culture. Two currents flow through this alliance. The first is dominated by Israel and thus is destined to be associated with specific political choices, which have been mostly on the conservative side. The second, not necessarily made up of different people, is highly sensitive to its own past and its history of a type of solidarity that carries anything but conservative implications. So there is the moral issue, which European jargon would place on "the left," and there is the political question on "the right." This contrast is every bit as typical in Israel, and whether one side or the other prevails always depends greatly upon international events. Nevertheless, it is unlikely that neo-Christian Zionism will ever truly capture even the conservative side of Jewish American opinion, not to mention its liberal factions.

The list of possible conflicts must include the black churches. Despite the countless associations, aggregations, and denominations that diversify this church group, they are all inevitably dominated by the historically influential necessities of community representation and protecting the black masses. In strictly religious and theological terms, there are surprising affinities between neo-Christianity and the waves of religious revival that have inundated the black community. But even in this area, group and community interests pose insurmountable barriers. In addition there is the new Christian exclusion of blacks, or at least its accent on whiteness.

Thus the roadside is littered with signs of conflict and fragmentation. When Catholics and Jews living in large urban areas subject to deterioration and danger face such immediate social issues as housing, schooling and employment, their opinion and their mood may show a hint of racisim. But the Catholic hierarchy maintains strong moral leadership over its people, and the same is true of Jewish communities, so that neither is likely to allow conflict over basic moral value, least of all respect and tolerance of other groups. Inevitably, there is a moment when the people flock to the church. If and when such an event occurs, the bond between Catholics, Jews, and black churches will be reestablished, forming one of America's cultural poles. The other pole, as separate and as different as any pole is from its opposite, will be the new Christian conservative coalition. The fact that this movement is mentioned alongside the great spiritual movements of America shows the extent of what is occurring in fundamentalist Protestantism. But it also expresses the explosive and controversial character of the new movement. Tensions and contradictions that cannot materialize in politics can burst into existence in the names of the many churches, or in the name of a different way to interpret the meaning of church, spiritual need, and the rights and duties of religion. The question American churches will one day have to answer is whether the median line of culture has moved so far away from the rest of the world that it now resembles the apocalyptic and nonnegotiable demands of white neo-Christian fundamentalism, or if it still identifies with Catholic ecumenism, mainstream Protestant tolerance, Jewish cultural internationalism, and black solidarity.

When the combination of ceasefires, alliances, and occasional convergences that has marked the onset of the eighties begins to deteriorate, then we will see out-and-out confrontation between the different ways of expressing religious feeling. In historical, not literal terms, this will be a war of the churches.

THREE

A New Millenarianism

STUDENTS of theology and historians of religion will probably remember March 8, 1981, as a landmark day in relations between American Catholicism and Protestantism. On that occasion, the two most influential religious communities, the Catholics and the Episcopalians, celebrated mass and communion together in Norfolk, Virginia, declaring a mutual desire to unite their two churches while maintaining some of the theological characteristics that distinguish one from the other. Of course, historians of religious movements will explain that despite the seeming audacity of this innovation, it was actually only a natural and logical consequence of theological evolution. The ongoing convergence of Episcopalian and Catholic churches in America is as well known—and some say inevitable—as the corresponding rapprochement of Catholics and Anglicans in England and the recent reevaluation of Lutheranism by Roman Catholic theologians.

Sociologists of religious movements find several points of interest in the Norfolk event. The Catholic and Episcopalian churches, along with other "establishment" denominations and churches that help make up America's social fabric, feel threatened by the intense aggressive fervor of continually emerging new churches, new religions, new preaching, new cults, and new pastors. These new movements know no historical bounds or psychological restraints, and they have no recognized cultural or intellectual credentials. Their frenzy imposes itself in the form of an absolute demand that expresses a combination

of exaltation and fear. Some of these churches seem to follow
the classic lines of Protestant evangelical preaching. Others are
under the forceful charismatic spell of individuals who come forth
to dominate crowds. Still others are a mixture of religion and
politics, or they blend religious behavior with immediate and
precise secular goals. Some answer a need for solidarity, some
for defense, and others for a space apart from every other space,
while still others come from deep mistrust and real fear. The
sense of doomsday, the persuasion that the end is inevitable and
a new birth is salvation, seem to pervade most of these new
cults.

The cultural perception of doomsday that exists within the
vast network of American neo-Christian movements is the
product of subjective moral persuasion. The new cults do see
themselves as the harbingers of the millennium, and this makes
them capable of aggressive behavior that is totally devoid of the
social reserve so common to churches at other moments in history. The neo-Christians are inclined to express their stubborn
watchfulness in ominous warnings of impending doom. But this
extreme frenzy and terror of approaching disaster, which justify
even the most dramatic reactions, are not limited to Christian
culture alone.

On March 4, 1981, a Hasidic Jewish neighborhood in New
York City was visited by Grand Rabbi Yisucher Dov Rokeach,
the spiritual leader of the Belz sect. His arrival created an
emergency for the New York Police Department, which saw itself forced to protect the rabbi and his entourage as they might
a head of state during a revolution. The other leading Hasidic
faction, the Satmar, had not only reacted violently to the Belz
"invasion," but had geared up to assault the rabbi or even, the
police suspected, to assassinate him. During Rabbi Rokeach's
visit the entire Williamsburg district swarmed with bomb squads
searching for explosives and weapons. Ambulances came and
went, intensifying the state of alarm. Arli Goldman of the *New
York Times* wrote that "the Belz and Satmar sects stem from a
common . . . tradition that emphasizes religious observance
through ecstasy, mysticism, and fierce loyalty to a grand rabbi."

The issue that has locked the sects in bitter opposition is the Messiah. The Belz believe that the state of Israel should be a reality before the coming of the Messiah, while the Satmar consider this heretical, because they believe the existence of a Jewish state is sacreligious as long as the Messiah has not been heard. But it is not theological differences that should attract our attention. It is the mystic extremism and the physical violence of the two groups who, the New York police say, are "capable of anything," evidently in defense of their interpretation of historical events. This outlook is every bit as fanatical and extreme as neo-Christian fervor.

In turn, experts of religious events would say neo-Christianity is not so dissimilar to the behavior of so-called Jewish defense groups, such as those led in America (and now in Israel) by Rabbi Meir Kahane or Rabbi Levinger, which preach and practice physical violence, assault, and terrorist acts. Like its American counterpart, Israel's traditionally pragmatic and moderate government took a brusque religious about-face between 1979 and 1980, when the pressure of small but active minority groups forced it to accept the principle of "divine possession of a land for the people of Israel." This resulted in the policy of increasing settlements in the occupied territories, which implied disregard for the complex international problems this would create and the threat to peace it would entail.

But this new religious interference with politics and public affairs is actually only the tip of a much broader iceberg. It was not until one Chester Bitterman was assassinated in Colombia that Americans learned of the hundreds of missionaries who had "invaded" that wartorn and terrorist-riddled Latin American country. In Bogotá alone there are 2,000 Christian missionaries, whose sole purpose is to translate the Bible into the various local *indios* dialects in order to convert the *campesinos* with readings from its texts. Bitterman, still in his twenties when he was killed, worked for a center whose name, the Summer Institute of Linguistics, had persuaded both Colombia and the United States that it was involved in university research. Any one who respects the traditional idea of a missionary's function would certainly be surprised to learn that, despite the tragic conditions existing in Colombia, the Summer Institute was and still is exclusively dedicated to the translation and distribution of such Bibles as the version inspired by the Calvary Fundamentalist Church of Lancaster, Pennsylvania, or the edition of the Wycliffe Bible Translator Institute in Huntington Beach, California. These "missionaries" have never shown concern or involvement in social assistance, nutrition, education, or any other improvement of local living conditions.

"We know our life is in danger," eulogized missionary Robert Pittman, who performs the same translating and preaching duties in the Philippines, "but it is imperative that the Word of God reach directly and immediately to those who have never heard it. God knows what he is doing, and he has just begun his work." These circumstances hint that the outbreaks of religious passion to which the Western world is being exposed are entirely similar to the storms of Islamic fundamentalism, despite widely varying economic and historical conditions.

THE NEW MISSIONARIES

The inflexible urgency of fundamentalist faith has brought the new missionaries face-to-face with a problem of which they seem to be totally unaware. The cultural alienation under which they operate is so serious that they are often accused, as they were in Colombia, of espionage or child exploitation. Indeed, the guerrillas in Colombia immediately withdrew their claims to Bitterman's assassination when they learned that he was "only a missionary." After seeing Bitterman and his young associates roam from village to village in search of some means to communicate and observing their complete indifference for the living conditions around them, the rebels never dreamed that the Americans might be church workers. But the dire urgency behind this millenarianism can make violence acceptable, compromise or negotiation impossible, and interest in circumstances and conditions, be they historical or local, superfluous.

What is more, the Guayana tragedy, in which Jim Jones' followers committed collective suicide in Jonestown in 1978, shows that this millenarian sense of urgency and crisis is far more widespread and deep-rooted than either educated or common belief might normally think.

Another tragedy exploded in 1981, but the chain of events to which it belonged went back at least to 1978. When dozens of black youths and children were killed in Atlanta, the tragedy brought the latent but intense millenarianism of many black churches to light. Child murder, as a sign of "the day of Last Judgment," is a theme that has often appeared in black preaching, despite the steady efforts ot black leaders and civil rights heirs, from Atlanta's Mayor Andrew Young to Coretta King, to channel the wave of emotion into solidarity and to use religious belief as a means for social improvement. But people like King and Young are themselves perceived as part of the establishment. Black fundamentalism, like its white counterpart, refuses to compromise or form alliances; it requires absolute faith and espouses nonnegotiable conditions. This fundamentalism is politically weaker than the white version, because the most active energies of the American black movement are still committed to a cooperative, solidaristic outlook. But its ability to contaminate, expand, and radicalize sentiment to extremist levels should not be overlooked. It is easy to see that the black movement can foment political militancy, which may even be characterized as "radical" or "liberal." But the spirit behind that liberalism is likely to be a tenacious fundamentalism, with its inevitable sense of urgency, drama, and impending finality. In other words, its millenarianism.

THE GOD OF CATASTROPHE

The doomsday sense of urgency and drama justifies and may even motivate extremist behavior, and it cannot be explained in the context of any one sect or movement. If this were an isolated phenomenon, it could easily be called group deviation.

But there are too many indications that it is not isolated. One example is the new political fundamentalism, which has the same impatient feelings of doom as religious millenarianism. For this reason, the antecedents must be sought in history and in social life and, above all, beyond the immediate realm of religion. If such attitudes are to be generally understood and widely tolerated, they must be preceded by cataclysmic conditions, fears, threats, insecurity, and confusion. Ideally, these conditions ought to be universally acknowledged; if they are not, they should at least be announced widely and regularly. In this sense, the neofundamentalist churches have had fertile ground in which to plant their seeds, and they have managed to nurture those seeds into the feeling of anxiety that now pervades the new cults.

Catastrophe in the Media. The mass media have always had a predilection for the negative, the tragic, and the threatening. Of course there are technical reasons for this, inasmuch as the news is more effective if it is larger than life. Spliced together, the montage of scenes may suggest a horizon strewn with disasters that can easily be interpreted as "blights" or "plagues."

The cataclysm suggests God's extreme punishment on the one hand and on the other a type of existence that is dangerous because it is running wildly out of control. Because it seems impossible to bring political control to bear upon a catastrophe of such dimension, faith may seem to be the only effective response. Thus in certain cultural and social conditions television, which usually widens the horizons of the common man's knowledge, can become a means to gather the masses around a few inviolable articles of faith. These, in turn, provide an interpretation of situations that would otherwise not be explicable; they help to alleviate panic and they compensate for mistrust in politics. What is more, it seems that passionate faith can fulfill the rational need for explanations and remedies. It does this by responding that a catastrophe is a punishment and by guaranteeing that the fight against sin will be rewarded by the light of truth, which will one day bring order where there is now only chaos.

Cultural Pessimism. Although light years removed from the pockets of backward subculture that are usually assumed to provide fertile ground for neo-Christianity, the most prestigious sources of culture and science paint just as coherent and gloomy a picture of the present and our possibilities for the immediate future. Rarely have the prognoses of culture and science been so frequently negative. The galloping improvements brought to everyone by technology over the past three decades have slowed to a limp, and this is now aggravated by the deficiencies of nature, from oil to grain and, in some parts of the world, even water. Science has never seemed so unprepared and ambiguous with respect to vital issues. Obviously, we are speaking of the way the mass media present science and culture. But what other source of information does the general public have? Clearly, the point is not whether the feeling of "damnation" has authentic scientific foundations. Even the literary, journalistic, philosophical, and sociological production of humanist culture seems to be right in line with the doomsday approach. Because politicians come from this same fertile ground, only two choices are open to them. If they accept, they will be adding their voices to expressions of pessimistic prophecy. Of course they can deny, but then they had better be blessed with a high degree of anticultural and antiscientific charisma. Something of which the new fundamentalist leaders seem to have plenty.

Social Fear. Thus a series of rapidly occurring incidents has apparently had negative consequences on daily life, the most important of which has been the spread of fear. Cities are overpopulated; bureaucracy and planning are often faulty; communication is uncertain, be it long-distance mail or short-run urban mass transit; one's home turf is rife with social conflict and tension; common criminality is everyday and everyone's experience; control of the family erodes; relations with one's own children are a thing of the past; drugs and the collapse of public authority bring clamorous but unclear modifications in social mores. All this combines to produce wild shifts in public behavior, as expressed in two phenomena seem more and more frequently. First, large masses which would normally be careful and judicious are induced to cross over into the adventure of violating the law. Indeed, compared with today's reality, adventure is no longer as risky and terrifyingly uncertain as it once was. Second, the general public has the urge to replace its traditional political leadership, whether institutions or men, with something strong enough to withstand the collapse thought to be occurring on all fronts. Only the most fervid and absolute form of religion can fulfill this need. Even when the new doomsday feeling is unconscious, it germinates and grows if social pacts are broken. It is especially tenacious within the part of the public that wants to reinvest its trust but shuns the institutions that have disappointed it. Because these people need absolutes, their reference point must be God, and their relationship with God must be inflexible.

The Culture of Self. During the seventies, America began to be overrun with an obsessive concern for the self as opposed to the group or social environment. For the most part, this has been interpreted as an equally strong but inverse response to the fervid social involvement of the preceding decade. This attitude contains no religious overtones per se. It is expressed in a series of behavior patterns that range from keeping in physical shape to self-improvement to mind expansion, all of which are aimed at making the person a better individual. "Treat yourself as if you were your own child" is the slogan of the culture of Self. And indeed, the birth rate has dropped dramatically, the divorce rate is dramatically increasing, social life is more and more oriented to the needs of the single person. The culture of Self has produced its own fiction, thanks to such authors as Ann Beattie and Susan Cheever; literature written by people alone for people alone; a limitless supply of self-improvement books; its own sociology, as voiced in Christopher Lasch's *The Age of Narcissism;* and its own secular churches. For several years, its most popular and active center was the est Institute, whose leader, Werner Erhardt (actually a German pseudonym), claims to have reached no less than twelve million Americans.

The new narcissism can be defined as the secular, sociological, or cultural conditions that provide, among other things, the setting for a rigorously individual kind of quasi religion that never asks its followers to give unto others but recommends severity, punishment, discipline, and clear-cut limitations of any "social" activity. This kind of belief can be experienced as a protective container that keeps its flock untouched by fearsome collective life, simplifying incomprehensible problems. It is one more link to the desire to find indisputable answers for oversimplified problems by secure authority, having nothing to share with traditional culture, science, or churches.

Survivalism. Recently, this term has cropped up more and more often in American publications. It stands for a series of solutions, ranging from the practical (weapons) to the protective (food and safe refuge) to the economic (how to change insecure cash into objects of certain value) to the instructional (self-defense). Although most of the training courses, books, and centers are directed at family groups rather than at individuals, survivalism is just another individual self-protection technique. Based upon solitude, it is motivated by distrust of institutions and the pervasive feeling that man lives as an island and other men are his enemies. Judging by the sales of how-to manuals dealing with terrorism or guerrilla warfare, muggers or the atomic bomb, monetary collapse or the destruction of the cities, this theme must have had enormous impact upon the imagination of America.

Survivalism is a series of secular techniques with no apparent

links to faith or religion. But in this case as in the others, the
motivation is supplied by a catastrophic or apocalyptic outlook
and by fear of imminent collapse, which lead to expectations
that undoubtedly encourage the development of religious millenarianism.

RELIGIOUS BELIEF AND THE TERROR OF THE UNKNOWN

America's new religious revival can only be analyzed and
understood in a larger social and historical context. Along these
lines, it might be useful to make three observations: first, to
establish the risks and values of this new belief; then, to examine the new galaxy of "semichurches" and look at the organizations which call themselves churches although they have little
or nothing to do with religion; third, to retrace several important steps in the historic development of new religion and neo-
Christianity.

In the first place, the collection of historical, social, cultural,
and political facts proposed as "fertile ground" for the new
doomsday approach should not only be interpreted negatively.
In other words, there are also positive connotations to the intense new demand for religion that much of the American public seems to be expressing. This demand is a people's response
to its own history and to the crisis it feels is undermining civic
and political affairs and traditional secular values. Thus the
steadily growing search for religion seems to contain one aspect
of stability and another of upheaval, and as it spreads it invests
every aspect of daily life with its own particular values. It is the
motivation behind commitments and the search for solutions; it
creates a shield to ward off the indifference and cynicism that
are seemingly endorsed by the worlds of politics and culture.

The religious reader might find this interpretation and its inherent evaluation limited to a few conveniences and practical
goals. Undoubtedly, the return to religious fervor and the search
for spirituality in America are important warnings that should
not be overlooked by sociologists and historians of culture. Nor

should this be dismissed as mere compensation for the anxiety that has resulted from technological, political, and economic crisis. It is also the expression of a need that overreaches the present limitations of secular culture, with its ambivalence, its facile capitulation, its ephemeral certainties, and its "noble" goals that so many times prove to be worthless.

The breadth of America's social landscape, the enormity of its dilemmas in times of strife, the dream or fulfillment of its triumph, its primal alientation from philosophical speculation and ideologically inspired responses: all these conditions can create a need for religion. History evolves and bureaucratical, industrial, technological, and international complications arise; then the search for the most intense religion of them all becomes the only way to find absolute answers. But the absolute nature of the religious response does not necessarily lead to authoritarian fundamentalism, just as it is not only a conservative phenomenon. Jim Jones, the suicide preacher of Guayana, was certainly on a doomsday course of catastrophe and apocalypse. His fundamentalist rigor was entirely similar to the fervor of some neo-Christian churches behind the Moral Majority's conservative front. And yet, Jones dreamed of mass migration to the Soviet Union; he sought Cuban support and felt persecuted by the CIA. Like the neo-Christians, Jim Jones was not adverse to the use of arms, nor did he shrink in the face of violence. His tenets of absolutism were not incompatible with death, whether as punishment given or received, or as the extreme solution.

Thus the absolute can be violent and authoritarian independently of local political connotations. It is always a danger when it shows up in valueless and faithless surroundings; or when the worshipers of "absolute value" can be persuaded that they are living in conditions of emergency and impending danger. This is probably the best setting for an explanation of religious fundamentalism when it invades political territory: an absolute, rigorously internal religious need is transformed into a peremptory demand that must be imposed upon society as a whole.

THE RELATIONSHIP BETWEEN CHARITY AND FAITH

There is another criterion that may explain the differences be-tween equally intense religious demands destined to emerge in radically different forms. It goes back to the history of religion and the development of Christianity, and it has heavily influ-enced the many forms of Christian preaching and worship that have existed in America. In Christian spirituality, there are two values which go hand in hand, one aimed at establishing exter-nal relations and the other at founding and defending inner in-tegrity. These two values are charity and faith, which Catholic teaching raises to the theological status of "virtues," associating them with hope and thereby predisposing them to a social out-look directed toward the future, progress, and a very human belief in the opportunity for improvement. Charity and faith are the two focal points of Christian teaching. Entire chapters of Christian spirituality have been dramatically affected by the equilibrium and conflict between these two values.

The masses that flocked to support civil rights rallied to a cry of charity, better defined as "compassion" in American reli-gious jargon. Fundamentalism and evangelicalism have always flown the flag of faith. But when the intensity of faith cannot become mystical inward exploration, it turns into a social force that is inversely proportionate to charity. This explains the hundreds of Bible translators who risk their lives to teach the memorized Word to *indios* living in far-flung villages along the Andes; it explains their lack of interest in the Indians' physical needs. On the contrary, these "missionaries" are disturbed by reform, perhaps because they interpret it as undesirable inter-ference with a form of reality ruled directly by God. Another thing this explains is the nonnegotiability of the conditions pro-posed by fundamentalism and by the evangelical preaching of neo-Christianity. The movement looks backward, and is thus conservative, because when faith is divorced from charity there is no longer any need for realistic relations with history.

In America, two great religious reserve forces have formed along this demarcation line. Both are motivated by disappointment in politics, technology, and science. But one of them calls for salvation through solidarity, and this is represented by Catholicism, mainstream Protestantism, and most of Jewish culture and religion. The other demands absolute faith, and it will allow no personal or social obstacle to keep this theological principle from complete fulfillment.

Is it a coincidence that this religious outlook has forged a political connection with the new secular conservatism. The front that has resulted is a conglomeration of socially and culturally marginal churches that feels it is now invested with temporal power. Historians are all too familiar with the dangers of such contamination. It is no coincidence that the demand for absolute and exclusive faith and the abandonment of charity have happened at the same time that a sense of danger, emergency, and doomsday has blossomed. As we have seen, there are countless forms of secular culture based upon solitude, narcissism, and self-care, and these inevitably lead to a *sauve qui peut* attitude. All of this has combined to make a fertile setting for a religious absolutism that has nothing to offer and everything to ask; requires fixed images instead of historical evolution, simple explanations rather than analysis of complications; and will not hesitate to sacrifice any or everything to its absolute tenets of salvation.

THE SPREAD OF THE SEMICHURCHES

This is no new phenomenon, but it has snowballed since the demise of the sixties-culture communes, which produced a wide range of cults from the mellow solidarity of Monterey and Carmel to the tragic brutaility of the Manson family. After this trend had thoroughly infiltrated its home territory, it resurfaced again in closely corresponding cultures like Synanon, or in other forms like the Granville phenomenon, which were incredibly different and remote. Whichever the case, this sort of cult always came complete with the motifs of the church, pastor, faith, and discipline.

Synanon began in California as a drug treatment center under the charismatic leadership of Chuck Dederich. How an institute for mutual aid could have been transformed into a tough, closed, repressive organization based upon absolute power, physical violence, cruelty, arbitrary judgment, and the violation of rights and laws is a mystery that has been resolved only partially by countless judicial and media inquiries. But the important factor here is the passage from charity- or compassion-based solidarity to authoritarianism, probably through a process in which the demands of obedience and faith gradually came to outweigh the human needs and interests of the group.

Another interesting example is a group that calls itself The Circle of Friends, actually several hundred women who live together in a small New Jersey town. Everyone's activities gravitate around the circle: all earnings are pooled, and every move in life depends upon the "advice" and "guidance" of the group. Like Synanon, the circle has been the object of numerous judicial and media investigations. But despite doubts of every kind, the circle has never yet been broken. Its wealth is still unknown and it is still unknown how the "circle" maintains power over its "friends." It is not even clear whether its "advice" and orders are within the limits of the law.

Charles Glock and Robert Bellah (*The New Religious Consciousness*, 1976), an authoritative research project on the new religious conscience in America, say there is one important fact to keep in mind when exploring the American religious landscape. Since the nineteenth century, when Mary Baker Eddy founded the Christian Science Church, whose members simply call it "the science," American religion and parareligious culture has shown little interest in a clear-cut distinction between science and faith. Any aspect of contemporary culture can therefore become the raw material for new forms of religion. This trend is even more evident among the myriad "quasi re-

ligions" which are an important historical and psychological link
in the chain of facts that explains America's new religious season.

RELIGIOUS REVIVALS IN AMERICAN TRADITION

Now and then a historical moment comes along and sets off a
string of intense religious revivals that generate new cults. In
America, the drama, transition, insecurity, and disorientation
that seem to foster new forms of spirituality have never been a
reflection of international events. They have always been a consequence of internal tensions. For instance, the thirties were
affected less by the tragedy of Europe than by the Depression.
And later, it was the explosion of the counterculture and not
the Vietnam crisis that put an end to the sixties. Today, politics
seems to be shifting from left to right; social patterns from collective commitment to individual concerns; culture from the big
cities and large universities to the small town and rural setting;
generations from the young to the middle-aged; and economy
from the very rich or the very poor to the middle class. In the
same fashion, religion seems to be moving from bizarre sects
like the Church of Satan to a reburgeoning of traditional faiths
like Christian Science, the Seventh-Day Adventist Church, and
the Jehovah's Witnesses; and from the language of the sixties
as expressed by the Christian World Liberation Front to the
austere conservatism of the Moral Majority.

The most interesting aspect of this transition is the unprecedented involvement of the Catholics, as witnessed in such
movements as the Catholic Charismatic Renewal, and of a fair
amount of young Jews, as in the "Jews for Jesus" movement.
On November 25, 1983, *Time* magazine carried a full-page ad-
vertisement on the Jews for Jesus movement and the same ad
was printed in mass circulation dailies and weeklies all over the
country. In 1984, the authoritative *Jewish Week–American Examiner* felt compelled to address the issue and sound the alarm
at least three times: January 6, March 2, and March 23. Jewish

scholars such as Trude Weiss-Rosmarin even proposed the institution of a cultural society belt to contain Christian missionary infiltration into young Jewish groups in schools and universities. In addition, real fanatacism has exploded in the Jesus cults, which have almost entirely alienated themselves from the theological and liturgical contexts of the Protestant and Catholic churches.

While the Catholic Charismatic Renewal shares many of the features of neo-Christianity, it is unique in that it started in 1967, sometime before most of the Protestant movements began to revert to fundamentalism. Indeed, it was originally called the Catholic Pentecostal Movement and, like many neo-Christian congregations, it was an outgrowth of the intense faith that is expressed in miracle worship. The movement was founded by two young theology teachers at Duquesne University in Pittsburgh, who took a vow to pray uninterruptedly until they had both been visited by the Holy Ghost. Finally, in January 1967, they were both "sure" they had been "filled" with the Spirit, which had given them the "gift of tongues" and preaching. By 1973, with guarded support from the Jesuits of San Francisco, the movement had more than 100,000 followers, and its missionaries had spread throughout the United States and (they say) into twenty foreign countries.

It was quick to establish ties with Protestant pentecostal groups; such being the case, it has never been completely clear why the hierarchy of the American Catholic Church accepted it. Particularly since it steadily acquired all the characteristics of fundamentalist Protestantism, such as definite anti-intellectualism, despite the movement's own academic origins; tacit but no less precise restrictions regarding social and ethnic background, meaning virtually no black and exclusively middle-class recruitment; an un-Catholic lack of interest in social assistance, charity, or solidarity; literal interpretation of faith and blind acceptance of the ineffable nature of the miracle; and a refusal to explain how, why, or in what form the Spirit shows itself, except to constantly refer to a "state of joy." The analogy that exists between the Catholic Church's behavior toward the new pentecostalists and the Protestant church's treatment of the Jesus cults suggests that both church organizations hoped to rely upon apparent dogmatic and formal affinities such as the Holy Spirit and the image of Jesus to keep the new movements in line with their parent churches as they spread.

The all-inclusive term "Jesus movement" might be used to describe the countless religious groups that have been inspired over the past fifteen years by the "personality cult" of Jesus Christ. Like the pentecostalists, these cults soon manifested mistrust of culture and intellectuals, alienation from mainline institutions, and blind faith in the "mystique of the experience." The "experience" in this case is every bit as ineffable as the feeling of being "filled" by the Holy Spirit. It is the "experience of Jesus," and it implies a definite rejection of the traditional caution practiced by both Catholics and Protestants. Oddly enough, this experience and the refusal to have any kind of dialogue with those who had not had or did not intend to have it both came to the Jesus movement by way of the drug culture. Often in the sixties, when young addicts were asked to discuss their drug problem, they would defend themselves by challenging the nonuser to try drugs first. The same attitude and inflexibility reappeared in the demand to "experience Jesus" and the refusal to have any contact with groups, churches, or believers who did not desire or accept that experience.

Mainstream Protestant resistance to the various nuances of the Jesus movement was as weak as Catholic response to the pentecostalists. On the other hand, Billy Graham, who represented a cautious traditional variety of evangelicalism, welcomed these cults with open arms. But soon the movement dumped Graham in favor of a more "pure" form of evangelism; that is to say, one less tainted by theology and closer to the emotional and psychic experience of the miracle. So the mainstream churches and even the charismatic preachers were rejected, and it seems they miscalculated the situation.

The movement's new Jesus was anticultural, antiestablishment, and the movement should have been promptly rejected by the professionals of religious life. According to Donald Heinz, author of many studies on America's religions, the American mass cult's Jesus went through two phases corresponding to two social and cultural stages in American life. The first phase begot the slogan, "Jesus is one of us," justifying even the most doubtful of alternate life-styles characterized by protest. During the second, the Word was "to belong to Christ" or "to be one of Christ's people," which demonstrated the conservative swing toward more traditional individual positions. Because these movements encouraged mistrust of the political and religious establishments, the new mass of followers drifted toward evangelicalism and the Baptists and, as the American political climate began to change, toward fundamentalism.

The Jesus of the feverish youth cults never possessed any theological reference points; because it always operated outside normal Christian tradition, it was only natural that the movement would eventually congeal into one of the most exalted and inflexible celebrations of religious feeling. At the same time, these were the least highbrow and most hard-core of all the cults. With such groups as Jews for Jesus, the movement grew until it claims millions of members all devoted to the most frenzied and passionate, least rigorous forms of neoevangelism and neofundamentalism. This was an unprecedented victory for American Protestantism's least intellectualized faction. The key phrases "Jesus has yet to arrive" or "Jesus is on his way" helped to keep fresh human material streaming into the torrent of messianic fever founded upon absolute faith in the miracle, sudden revelation of the Holy Ghost, and "the gift of tongues," however incomprehensible to many that might be. This newborn throng of believers eventually found themselves in the ranks of fundamentalist Protestantism when it became clear that it embodied purity and absolute faith and could provide a miraculous response to the fear that was mounting within the other mass followers of America's new religions, causing them to mistrust and shun secular politics. And so the doomsday formula was created, and it gave the neo-Christians self-appointed authority to try to impose their beliefs upon the political establishment. During the 1980 elections, the media was blitzed by a broad-based provincial and peripheral mass movement strong enough to infiltrate Congress and even stake a claim to the White House.

Although this is not the first time such a situation has occurred in the United States, these movements had never before received public support from the very heart of the political world. As we have seen, there is obviously a great deal of resemblance between America's new Christian doomsayers and many waves of neo-fundamentalism that are shaking large areas and nations of the world. So these events seem neither isolated, coincidental, nor fleeting, and this seems to be just the beginning.

FOUR

To the Right and to
the Left of God

THERE are many ways to subdivide American religion into
categories to understand its meaning and importance, predict
future developments within the religious movements, and fore-
see the way they will interfere with and affect politics. Com-
parisons might pit the mainstream Protestant denominations,
Catholicism, and Judaism against the new movements; or establishment churches against increasing demands for new forms
of spirituality; or the cults of inner fervor against the movements of social mobilization and organization; or preservation
groups against reform groups; or the relationship between faith
and culture against a radical rejection of daily reality, in favor
of exceptional circumstances and absolute peremptory faith in
salvation through the miracle.

The evangelical and fundamentalist movement reinforces the
Protestant tendency toward fragmentation and the formation of
new sects. With its renewed fervor, militancy, and organization, it seeks a return to the past and eschews exploration of
the possibilities inherent in a new and different future. The new
movements are strongly conservative in their politics and theology, so that today's call for change, renewal, and acceptance
of new social situations comes almost exclusively from older
churches and religious cultures.

The importance of the charismatic leader also distinguishes

the new religions from the old, and this is true even when the newcomers look to the extreme left, as was the case with the Guayana People's Temple. At the same time, solidarity and compassion continue to characterize the establishment churches and religious institutions. Last, the great Judeo-Christian family tree has been drained by a numerically modest but culturally seductive and effective "flight to the East" and its religious teachings. Of course the term "flight" is to some extent a value judgment. But paradoxically, there seems to be some invisible link between the Eastern cult groups and the pentecostalists, the Jesus movemet, the charismatic miracle movements, and the new evangelist and fundamentalist churches. Naturally, such an allegation would be vigorously denied by all sides. But they do share a strongly anti-intellectual attitude; deep mistrust in institutions; a blatant, irreversible indifference toward the traditional relations that have always united church, culture, and social environment; and a profound sense of alienation and desire for separation from all of social organization. At first glance, it might seem that what distinguishes the Eastern cults from the neo-Christians is this determination to get out of the unspoken pact between religion and social affairs. Yet a significant portion of the evangelists, Jesus cults, pentecostalists, and miracle workers silently but defiantly have adopted this same attitude of self-segregation from public duties and responsibilities. Still, we must be careful to remember the cultural distinction between everything that comes out of the Judeo-Christian framework and the proliferating Oriental cults. Despite the behavioral and motivational affinities between many of the new church groups, there are practical differences, and even during their short existence in the United States, the gap has widened.

As we have seen, even within the Judeo-Christian culture there is an abyss between neo-Christianity and the mainstream churches. The new sects are disgruntled with the establishment churches' irreverent disrespect of literal Biblical tradition, which is how they interpret the accommodating "liberal" and "un-Christian" tolerance regarding the such issues as family morality, national defense, and numerous other nonnegotiable principles. Catholic and Jewish cultures are also exposed and susceptible to the explosions of neo-Christian fervor. As a result, there have been frequent changes of position, and alliances that form over one issue later explode over others, so that the situation has been one of creative but potentially dangerous tension.

Occasionally, groups operating outside Jewish and Catholic culture and religion are able to create a deep rift within these two religions over a commonly shared cause. This is what has occurred in the antiabortion crusade, the sensitive political nature of which has frequently clashed with such issues as peace, racial injustice, and defense of the poor, clearly liberal causes dear to many members of the antiabortion coalition and strange to others. At other times, contradiction seems touched off by theology, as when John Paul II renewed the abortion issue; or by historical or political causes, such as support for Israel. Because of these contrasts, it is exceedingly difficult to make political or cultural predictions regarding the future behavior and strategy of the various faiths.

Then there are the social effects, which make the future even more uncertain. Traditionally, Catholics and Jews have always been the most active part of the American middle class. They share that class's anxiety, fear, and uncertainty and they tend to express them politically, by shifting part of their weight, for instance, from traditional support for the Democratic Party to a new form of Republican militancy. This can have repercussions on delicate problems such as relations with racial minorities and the social, economic, occupational, and cultural implications of those relations, as well as on international policy. Clearly, some of these problems, such as the shift from one political party to another, are momentary. But another part lies buried deep within religious conscience, and it affects discipline, faith, orthodoxy, continuity, and tradition. It is this second aspect which should be most carefully examined.

THE CATHOLIC LEFT AND RIGHT

At the beginning of 1981, America's Catholic leadership found itself unexpectedly involved in a clash with the federal government. The incident, which grew out of the church's defense of the Maryknoll sisters, was also a rather explicit manifestation of the bitter underlying conflict that can exist between church and state. In this case, the immediate cause was the El Salvador assassination of several nuns belonging to the Maryknoll order; this was followed closely by the State Department's comment that the sisters were killed "in combat," suggesting they had been fighting with the rebels. But the real reason for the conflict was ongoing political torment in the small Central American republic. The American government interprets this revolution as a Communist plot, while Catholic leadership attributes it to serious social injustice. In the case of El Salvador, the United States and the Roman Catholic Church are two hegemonies competing on the same turf for the same reason, which is to protect their investments and patrimony. For the one the stakes are political allegiance and defense; for the other they are participation and leadership in Latin American Catholicism. Of course Rome will continue to temper the problems and choices of that Catholicism so that they fit in with the church's needs throughout the world, but it is certainly not willing to capitulate on the battlefield. And so, while the interests of the Catholic Church and the United States government are almost the same, the expressions of those interests have locked the opponents in an unexpected conflict. The Church supports solidarity with the people, if not directly approving their rebellion then at least protecting the poor and the unprotected among the people. The administration supports solidarity with established governments, giving their stability urgent priority over every other problem.

The church-state clash over the Maryknoll sisters was fierce; in the end, the Maryknoll order issued a point by point denial of all the State Department charges, even enlisting the involvement of congressmen and senators, which consequently called attention to the liberal-conservative polarization that exists on the church-state issue. Despite its brevity, it was a forceful episode; statements made before, after, and independently of the incident showed the Catholic leadership's basic values and priorities were not just different from but in opposition to the administration's.

As we know, localized Catholic militancy in favor of human rights, freedom for political prisoners, and the defeat of autocratic regimes, above all in the Philippines, Argentina, Chile, and South Africa, has been in part offset by John Paul II's position. In his very first public address, on the occasion of the 1978 Eucharist Congress in Mexico, the pope warned that the "theology of liberation" should be avoided. Nevertheless, in numerous speeches calling for human rights, official representatives of the church have continued to respect some of these goals. Even the pontiff himself voiced this opinion at the beginning of 1981 on the occasion of his visit to the Philippines. The Church hierarchy cannot ignore hundreds of millions of faithful believers who oppose their own governments, at least over several fundamental issues, even indirectly coming to blows with the United States international policies, at least after 1980. Thus within the context of recent U.S. history, the position of the Catholic Church has been a liberal one.

The most sensational proof of this liberalism came in late 1982, when a delegation formed at the National Conference of Catholic Bishops under Chicago's new archbishop, Joseph Cardinal Bernardin, initiated debate on the morality of nuclear arms. The Catholic Church in America formally expressed its position in the "Bishops' pastoral letter on war and peace," approved by the conference and published on June 9, 1983, under the title, *The Challenge of Peace: God's Promise and Our Response.*

Several passages of this declaration provoked debate, consensus, and bitter polemics, not only among Catholics but also in the political ranks and media of the entire world:

On Deterrence:

1. "In current conditions 'deterrence' based on balance, certainly not as an end in itself but as a step on the way toward a progressive disarmament, may still be judged morally acceptable. Nonetheless, in order to ensure peace, it is indispensable not to be satisfied with this minimum which is always susceptible to the real danger of explosion." (Pope John Paul II, Message to U.S. Special Session on Disarmament, No. 8; June 1982.)

2. No use of nuclear weapons which would violate the principles of discrimination or proportionality may be intended in a strategy of deterrence. The moral demands of Catholic teaching require resolute willingness not to intend or to do moral evil even to save our own lives or the lives of those we love.

3. Deterrence is not an adequate strategy as a long-term basis for peace; it is a transitional strategy justifiable only in conjunction with resolute determination to pursue arms control and disarmament. We are convinced that "the fundamental principle on which our present peace depends must be replaced by another, which declares that the true and solid peace of nations consists not in equality of arms but in mutual trust alone." (Pope John XXIII, "Peace On Earth," No. 113.)

On the Arms Race and Disarmament:

1. The arms race is one of the greatest curses on the human race; it is to be condemned as a danger, an act of aggression against the poor, and a folly which does not provide the security it promises. (Cf: The Pastoral Constitution, No. 81; Statement of the Holy See to the United Nations, 1976.)

2. Negotiations must be pursued in every reasonable form possible; they should be governed by the "demand that the arms race should cease; that the stockpiles which exist in various countries should be reduced equally and simultaneously by the parties concerned; that nuclear weapons should be banned; and that a general agreement should eventually be reached about progressive disarmament and an effective method of control." (Pope John XXIII, "Peace on Earth," No. 112.)

On the Use of Nuclear Weapons:

1. Counter-Population Use: Under no circumstances may nuclear weapons or other instruments of mass slaughter be used for the purpose of destroying population centers or other predominantly civilian targets. Retaliatory action which would indiscriminately and dispro-

portionately take many wholly innocent lives, lives of people who are in no way responsible for reckless actions of their government, must also be condemned.

2. The Initiation of Nuclear War: We do not perceive any situation in which the deliberate initiation of nuclear war, on however restricted a scale, can be morally justified. Non-nuclear attacks by another state must be resisted by other than nuclear means. Therefore, a serious obligation exists to develop morally acceptable non-nuclear defensive strategies as rapidly as possible. In this letter we urge NATO to move rapidly toward the adoption of a "no first use" policy but we recognize this will take time to implement and will require the development of an adequate alternative defense posture.

3. Limited Nuclear War: Our examination of the various arguments on this question makes us highly skeptical about the real meaning of "limited." One of the criteria of the just war teaching is that there must be a reasonable hope of success in bringing about justice and peace. We must ask whether such a reasonable hope can exist once nuclear weapons have been exchanged. The burden of proof remains on those who assert that meaningful limitation is possible. In our view the first imperative is to prevent any use of nuclear weapons and we hope that leaders will resist the notion that nuclear conflict can be limited, contained or won in any traditional sense.

On Promoting Peace:

1. We support immediate, bilateral, verifiable agreements to halt the testing, production and deployment of new nuclear weapons systems. This recommendation is not to be identified with any specific political initiative.

2. We support efforts to achieve deep cuts in the arsenals of both superpowers; efforts should concentrate first on systems which threaten the retaliatory forces of either major power.

3. We support early and successful conclusion of negotiations of a comprehensive test ban treaty.

4. We urge new efforts to prevent the spread of nuclear weapons in the world, and to control the conventional arms race, particularly the conventional arms trade.

5. We support, in an increasingly interdependent world, political and economic policies designed to protect human dignity and to promote the human rights of every person, especially the least among us. In this regard, we call for the establishment of some form of global authority adequate to the needs of the international common good.

For the first time in American history, and perhaps in many centuries of Catholic history, a religious position has expressed a passionate contradiction with the political position of its government. Over recent years, America's religious movements have seemed to acquire a vitality and autonomy that often puts them in a position to voice change in popular sentiment faster and more dramatically than any other social organization. But for this very reason, modern churches have crossed over onto controversial territory which they have previously tended to avoid.

As we have seen, this "leftward swing" within and around the Catholic and other mainstream churches has been countered by a headlong "rightward lunge." With its stands on abortion, the family, and birth control, the Catholic Church has been swept up in this lunge. Certainly, these positions reflect traditional Catholic dogma and teachings and do not indicate a move to the right per se. But because of them, millions of Catholics have begun to operate in close alliance with the Christian fundamentalists, who are the most vigorous incarnation of America's New Right. And in this sense the Catholic Church, as the most active part of the antiabortion, morality, and family crusade, is part of the New Right. A Catholic theologian might explain that we are dealing with two different areas, the social and the moral, and that therefore there is no contradiction. But theoretical positions blossom into practical policy.

One example is the "march for life," an organization linking Catholics with other Christian groups. The movement's jargon and slogans are part of a radicalism that the organizers do not hesitate to call "apocalyptic." The "march for life" denies the right to abortion for whatever reason, including rape, and it compares abortionist physicians to the Nuremberg criminals, even when they perform the operation for therapeutic reasons. In addition, it resolutely opposes any kind of sex education, which "only serves to accelerate sexual activity"; birth control instruction, which is "a free ticket to depravity"; and assistance for teenagers or underprivileged women needing abortion, because "there can be no relationship between murder and social

condition, and abortion is always murder." These remarks were
made by one of the movement's leaders, Nelly Gray, in a March
13, 1981, interview. The fact that most of the "march for life"
leaders come from the Catholic Church is less important than
it might seem, because no one group can greatly outdistance
such radicalism. What counts here is that the movement's messages are so similar to the ones issuing from Rome on the same
subject.

The "march for life" has no political affiliation; it expresses a
moral militancy with exclusively theological motivations. But a
march is a physical operation based upon organized action. In
this case, the action clearly reflects the combativeness of the
fundamentalist wing of Protestantism, for whom abortion is one
of the keystones of a strictly conservative construction of life and
politics. For years now the "march for life" has publically celebrated its cause on the streets of Washington, with the purpose of strongly influencing legislators; in this it hardly differs
from the lobbyists kept in Washington by every other interest
group. Since 1981, the movement has sent its leaders straight
to the White House, to insure that the antiabortion crusade become part of a specific political program. Similarly, the movement used the highly effective "baby killer" slogan in the 1980
election campaigns to defeat several senators and congressmen
"guilty" of having supported welfare assistance for women unable to pay a private physician for an abortion. The pro-life
Catholic militants were not intimidated by the political prestige
of the movement's liberal Democratic victims, who included at
least a dozen of the country's most prominent legislators. The
fact that the men they managed to eliminate from Congress were
also among the key representatives of an international liberalism that the Roman Church seems to support in every other
aspect of public activity did not stop the Catholic antiabortion-
ists, either.

Because of the antiabortion coalition, Catholic leaders hesitate to express their substantial differences of opinion with political and religious neoconservatism. Leading Catholic voices

still seemed opposed to their government's international stance and social domestic policies. But no one issue is capable of giving any political and cultural coherence to this conflict today. American Catholicism stands both to the right and to the left of the government, on one side demanding far more than the administration would like to offer (i.e., a constitutional amendment to equate abortion with murder, as opposed to an antiabortion law) and on the other resisting the State Department's policy in Latin America and opposing the nuclear arms question in a firm stand reminiscent of the old anti-Vietnam liberalism. The antiabortion stance aligns the Catholic Church with the conservative fundamentalist front and weakens its presence in domestic affairs. The second stance indicates the persistence of a Third-World-oriented culture which is quite distant from the administration's policy but also well-removed from the average sentiments of many American Catholics. Furthermore, by tenaciously sticking to the antiabortion campaign, the Church has eliminated public figures it needs to support and voice its other political positions.

Has their natural rejection of abortion caused America's Catholics to be manipulated by other entirely unrelated conditions? Has this led them far astray from their traditional positions and their historical place in society? Certainly, Catholics are more inclined to choose a stance on religious grounds than for political affiliation. In this sense, they seem willing to pay the price for their contradictions. This means losing valuable supporters of their social outlook in exchange for keeping the collaboration of those whose political position is different but whose moral and dogmatic stance is the same.

BETWEEN THE TEACHINGS OF ROME AND NEO-CHRISTIAN RECRUITMENT

Although the Catholics' traveling companions on the "march for life" belong to messianic and doomsday movements, they nevertheless seem quite pragmatic and cautious when it comes to relations between religion and politics. Immediately after the new Reagan administration's announcement of its Cabinet ministers, the Moral Majority publicly declared it would not investigate the private lives of the appointees, several of whom are divorced and some of whom live outside marriage. In a statement given to the Associated Press on March 19, 1981, the movement said it would conduct no personal censures as long as the administration's new members continued to respect firmly conservative principles.

So the Catholic Church now finds itself tipped to the right by new alliances with conservatives and fundamentalists on the issue of abortion. But it has been manipulated by other religious groups which require political allegiance in return for their support on moral issues relevant to Catholics. "Live any way you want to, but be conservative."

At the beginning of 1981, a document released in Rome underscored the contradictory nature of the stands taken by the American Catholic Church. Written by an Italian Catholic conference of bishops, the statement's political nature gained it wide coverage in American media and religious publications. In it the bishops declared, "the church considers any legislation favoring abortion to be a most serious offense to the primary rights of man and the divine commandment not to kill. It is our Christian duty to use any means so that civil law be unequivocally altered to include a real guarantee of the value of motherhood and to protect human life from the moment of its conception."

Careful examination shows that the statement is more cautious that the one released by the conservative and fundamentalist coalition which has enrolled American Catholicism in its antiabortion crusade. Furthermore, neither the Italian nor the American bishops ask that abortion be legally equated with murder, preferring to address the moral issue without calling for judicial consequences as the neo-Christians have. But just as the American Catholics' allies do not hesitate to invade the political arena with their religious militancy, they have likewise ignored the tacit limits Catholicism has drawn between theology and criminality. They are defending the same morality expressed in Catholic doctrine, but in requiring legislation they have carried it to far more radical social, practical, and political consequences.

The Catholic Church's fundamentalist allies would strongly object to the second part of the bishops' statement, which postulates a connection between two world visions. The fundamentalists want nothing to do with the bishops' disapproval of a programmed diffusion of the "death culture," which is how the Roman Catholic Church defines both the arms race and capital punishment. Here the Catholic position, which is certainly an expression of church dogma, differs sharply from the fundamentalist one. Indeed, Catholic doctrine rejects the "moral duty" of preserving superior military might and the death penalty, both of which are peremptory demands of the entire American conservative front and particularly of the New Christian Right.

America's Catholic Church may clash with liberal culture on some issues and with the conservatives on others, but it appears to be coherent when it comes to morality and theology. The problem of political direction and content is an entirely different one. Indeed, the inherent contradictions we have examined do not depend entirely upon the Church itself, being the reflection of another organization's agenda, the separate items of which each activate different parts of the Catholic population. This may be the first time in all the history of Catholicism that the Church has been manipulated by other religious movements whose doctrine is so far removed from its own.

Another factor is the traditional solidarity and social commitment of the Catholic Church in America. In a moment of such complex evolution and difficult decisions, the Church's communication with its congregation becomes all the more delicate. Still today, in the poor neighborhoods of a city like New York, the Catholic Church continues to devolve a large part of its means to "charitable works." A partial list of Catholic urban activities would surely include the seven hundred black nuns

who work in the most desolate ghettos of America, the most
famous and courageous of whom are the Franciscan Handmaids
of Mary, whose mother house is on 124th Street in Harlem.
Then there are Mother Teresa's sisters who work in the Bronx;
the charitable institutions; hospitals; daycare centers and homes
for Catholic women. According to Mother Miriam Cecilia of the
Handmaids, only 5 percent of the population in these poor
neighborhoods may be Catholic, but the waiting list for aid is
"unreal." The whole organization testifies to the persistence of
the essential teaching of charity among Catholics.

It is still unknown whether the tidal wave of neo-conservatism that has inundated America since the end of the seventies
has affected these traditional attitudes of American Catholics. It
is still uncertain whether they too have been touched by the
culture of self that has become the sign of the eighties; by the
neo-Christian type of religion that cries of doomsday and has
no interest in social work; or by middle-class anxiety and insecurity, with its demands for the death penalty and reassurance
of protection by force, its impatience with complicated foreign
politics and its downright scorn for the "rights" and demands of
the poor. This dual allegiance and superimposition of right upon
left have created a Catholicism that is at once powerful and vulnerable. Whether or not the church will be permanently weakened by this situation will depend upon the kind of bond that
exists between the hierarchy and the congregation.

AMERICA'S JEWS: CULTURAL IDENTITY AND POLITICAL
CHOICE

Sociologists and observers of American trends warn against
overrating the Moral Majority, evangelical conservatism, or
fundamentalism, with their nonnegotiable demands voiced in
the name of a seemingly vast public that has sprung from nowhere. The most authoritative disclaimer has come from *Commentary*, the American Jewish Committee's magazine, which
hoped with its comments to calm the mass-media furor it felt
had unjustly attributed responsibility for America's rightward

swing to the new Christians. In the article "The Election and
the Evangelicals," written soon after the elections, Seymour
Martin Lipset, professor of political science at Stanford University, and Earl Raab, executive director of the Jewish Community Relations Council of San Francisco, propose several interesting theories. They claim that the political and cultural roots
of this new conservatism actually reach far beyond the scope of
evangelicalism. They say that while evangelicalism and such recent fundamentalist offshoots as Moral Majority and the Committee for the Survival of a Free Congress have acquired conservative militancy, this activism does not necessarily typify the
neo-Christian movements, which may include factions that are
liberal or at least more liberal than the Moral Majority's coalition. In short, it was not evangelicalism that gave determinant
support to America's new conservatism.

These statements appear to have been made in understandable self-defense of political positions held by the two authors
and *Commentary*. The fact is that *Commentary*, its editor Norman Podhoretz, and intellectuals like Lipset are all among the
founders and theoretical formulators of the new conservatism.
They are justified in wanting to claim a lion's share of the
movement's cultural substance, philosophical perspective, and
political coherence; indeed, of its very creation. They did mobilize a remarkable pool of American resources and intellectual
talent from the moderate center and even from the ranks of the
left, transfusing it into the center-right coalition that contributed to the GOP victory in 1980. Later, that same brain pool
went on to support the Congress that resulted from those elections, even participating in the Reagan administration itself. But
Commentary, Podhoretz, Lipset, and Raab are first and foremost voices of the American Jewish Committee, which is the
outstanding political force in America's Jewish community. It
would appear that the Lipset–Raab report was inspired by the
same anxiety circulating in other sectors of the new conservative majority; which is to say, as we have already seen, among
Catholics and, as we shall soon see, among mainstream Protestants.

Can we really accept the opinion that the neo-Christian fundamentalist and evangelical groups are the advance guard or determining factor of a new political rank? And if so, what are the consequences to the identity and defense of other groups, particularly the Jewish component of the new alliance? Lipset and Raab choose to ignore such questions and concentrate on a flat denial. They claim that the neo-Christian movement is not so relevant politically for at least two reasons. One is that among neo-Christians not everyone is an ultra-conservative—for example, Jimmy Carter, a "born again" Christian. The second reason is that, according to Lipset and Raab, the political role of the neo-Christian movement in the 1980 election has been blown out of proportion by the media. Gallup, Harris, and ABC News polls supposedly show that the neo-Christians have not only not played a decisive role but that they have actually damaged some of the candidates they support. But Lipset and Raab draw upon data that were extrapolated from other contexts, and so their arguments have yet to be proven. For one thing, all of the candidates allegedly "damaged" by Christian support now hold seats in Congress, having replaced Church, Bayh, McGovern, Culver, Brademas, and other "enemies" of the coalition.

The *Commentary* essay mentions the great evangelical movement that raged through America before World War II. Led by the Reverend Gerald Winrod, the "jayhawk Nazi," that movement was definitely anti-Semitic by nature. But, say Lipset and Raab, Reverend Falwell of the Moral Majority was recently given an award by one Jewish organization, and Falwell has led his movement toward positions that he himself defines as "Zionist." The authors choose to overlook the "Family Protection Act" presented in Congress by Paul Laxalt, another member of the New Christian Front, which they say, "confines itself to fairly narrow questions" like school prayer and the right of parents to control and eventually censor school textbooks.

Now, both of these tranquilizing rationalizations can be disputed. Would the Reverend Gerald Winrod's anti-Semitism have ebbed naturally if World War II and its heavy anti-Nazism had not extinguished it? Is the simultaneous reappearance of anti-Semitism and the new Christian revival a mere coincidence, or is this discrimination inherent in the teachings and world outlook of Christian fundamentalism? Moreover, Jerry Falwell may have accepted the Jewish award as a political expedient. But why should any Jewish organization feel obliged to honor a fundamentalist, whose rigorous Christian vocation, within the context of recent Western history and its jargon, can only suggest the presence of discrimination against all that is not Christian? And would Falwell have been honored if he had been the leader of an insignificant group? Furthermore, it should be immediately apparent that it is a far cry from the Zionism that inspired Jewish culture to the Zionism championed by a rigorously Christian group with a history of discrimination and exclusion not only behind it but present in its very definition. In the latter case, "Zionism" may easily stand for a mass exodus of Jews to another country, for reasons that have nothing to do with Jewish history and culture.

As for the second allegation, how can it possibly be claimed that the Helms–Laxalt proposals for censorship of school textbooks and required Christian school prayer are "fairly narrow questions"? Cultural minority groups have never benefited from drives for unification, religious rigor, or confusion of the state-church relationship. The birth and proliferation of Christian schools, which the evangelical and fundamentalist groups have furiously defended as the only remedy for the "low Christian temperature of the public schools," should in themselves be a warning for America's Jewish culture.

Obviously, Lipset and Raab had other motivations when they wrote their article. On the religious and cultural front, the possibility of any threat is exorcised through a demonstration that the Moral Majority and its associates are irrelevant components in a political force of entirely different makeup. This is quite comprehensible, coming from two intellectual conservatives such as the authors, but when we consider that these same authors represent Jewish culture in America, it becomes less obvious.

They should be occupied not in identifying the organizational background of neo-Christianity but in assessing the movement's ability to affect American public opinion and upset the delicate balance between church and state. Where fundamentalist Christianity is concerned, this last point is of particular importance, because only by upsetting that balance can the cult grow freely and effectively disseminate its views and prejudices.

On the political front, Lipset and Raab draw upon the well-founded affirmations to the effect that a completely different set of circumstances led to the demise of the Democrats and the rise of the conservative Republicans. True. But one of these circumstances is this unprecedented alliance, which has left other authoritative Jewish intellectuals feeling anything but comfortably calm. The World Jewish Congress has been calling for a redefinition of Zionism. In the March 15, 1981, issue of the *Jewish Week and American Examiner*, Samuel Pisar discusses the recurrence of anti-Semitism throughout the world and in America; he proposes entirely new and different "natural" aliances, such as the one between blacks and the Jews. Arthur Hertzberg, president of the Jewish Policy Foundation and vice-president of the World Jewish Congress, has also written about the Moral Majority, and while he does not overrate its clout and effect, his assessment opposes the Lipset–Raab view. These three differing viewpoints furthermore only, show that no examination of neo-Christianity can stop at the statistics, and that the issue at stake includes far more than just the movement's strength.

ANXIETY AND REJECTION AMONG AMERICA'S JEWISH LEADERS

Now more than ever, debate in world Jewish culture centers around the redefinition of Zionism. Conflict was intensified in 1980 by a report attributed to incoming president of the World Jewish Congress Edgar Bronfman. The most unusual and controversial statement in the report was that "Zionism is no longer identified solely with leading the exiled people back to Israel." In other words, "Zionism cannot be synonymous with the settlement of every Jew in Israel." The extreme interest in terminology denotes the desire to assure a human, cultural, and political role for the Jewish community in every country of the world, regardless of that country's policies toward specific Israeli issues, except the ones of defense and survival. Many Jews fear that world Jewish culture might one day neglect the dream and reality of the Israeli state, or at least demote the issue from the central place it has always had as the fulfillment of a great historical and religious promise.

Whatever the case, creative and alive debate about the definition of Zionism demonstrates the facility (and thus the suspected opportunism) with which traditionally anti-Semitic American neo-Christians can now propose to support Zionism. Jewish debate about the concept and historical interpretation of Zionism restores center-stage status to several fundamental Jewish issues, among which are solidarity, the problems of social justice, and dialogue between Israelis and non-Israelis, Zionists and non-Zionists, Jews and non-Jews. This is all sufficient indication that the fundamentalist and evangelical proclamation of "Zionism," particularly when it comes from groups coordinated by the Moral Majority, appears more a political convenience than an expression of true moral persuasion or the expression of coincidental views.

The true gap between temporarily allied groups such as Jews and the new Christians would be more apparent if we listened to spokesmen whose political positions differ from those expressed by the magazine *Commentary*. In the March 2, 1981, issue of the Jewish Telegraph Agency's "Daily News Bulletin," Murray Zuckoff wrote, "Samuel Pisar is convinced that the resurgence of pernicious anti-Semitism is a worldwide reality and that no country is immune to this barbarism."

Pisar, a survivor of Auschwitz, is now a leading exponent of Jewish culture, whose remarks with regard to the new anti-

Semitism carry prestige and authority. "The seeds of collapse are sprouting everywhere. Those seeds are unemployment, inflation, economic uncertainty, the energy crisis, the uncertainty of oil supply, terrorism, violence in the streets and politicians who cannot cope, economists who cannot cope and diplomats who cannot cope. We are living in apocalyptical times. To me, we are facing quite possibly the thermonuclear gas chamber of the future—a kind of global Auschwitz." This viewpoint may not be held by the Jewish groups that honored Jerry Falwell, and it may contrast with the analysis proposed by neoconservatives Lipset and Raab in *Commentary*. Still, it is shared by a great many American and world Jews.

Pisar goes on to say:

There is a moment of confusion as to how to build alliances and with whom. My impression of the present time is that we [the Jewish people] don't know what to do about the basic question of how to prevent another Holocaust from ever happening again. The Jewish leadership doesn't know which way to jump. I think it is a tragedy that the old coalition between the Jews and the Blacks has come into question. I can understand how tactically such a thing could happen. But in terms of long-term strategy, of survival, of safeguarding the rights of the downtrodden, we Jews must never forget that we belong on that side.

Is the new Moral Majority friends, enemies, neutral? Should we be allied with these people, or are those the kind of people who ultimately represent a danger to us? In the long term, it's not a natural alliance. It's against the grain. I am afraid of these alliances because I don't know where they will end. Today a man like myself finds it very difficult to know who are the enemies and who are the friends. Where should we be and on whose side? Everything is tactical and from day to day. What is needed is thinking that is strategic. This is the survival.

With reference to the immediate problem of relations between Jews and neo-Christians, Rabbi Arthur Hertzberg writes with less alarmism but identical determination in the April 1981 issue of *Hadassah*:

As a Jew, I am not cheered by the support for Israel expressed by some of the major figures of the New Right. It is possible to be pro-

Israel for reasons which are either immediately or in the long run dis-
comforting for Jews. The more moderate Nazis were pro-Zionist in
the 1930's. They were willing to send the Jews to Palestine to "prove"
that the very willingness of those Jews to leave Germany showed that
"they were a different race."

For centuries, many Christian fundamentalists . . . have imagined
that helping the Jews to go to the Holy Land was the preamble to the
Second Coming and the conversion of the Jews. Some Christian Zionists of this stamp, as they wax enthusiastic about the return of the
Jews, also talk about the need, in the short run, to make the existing
Gentile society totally Christian. The Jews belong in the Holy Land—
and not in America.

The new Christian right is already talking, through the mouth of
Paul Weyrich, one of its leaders, of *"working to overturn the present
structure in this country; we are talking about Christianizing America."* Is this "good for Jews," or for America?

THE NEW RIGHT'S POLITICAL LOBBY

Paul Weyrich, who Hertzberg feels is a threat, is president of
the Committee for the Survival of a Free Congress, a powerful
neo-Christian lobby affiliated with the even more powerful and
respectable organization known as Religious Roundtable, an
umbrella structure that also includes the various factions of the
Moral Majority. An intensely active leader, Weyrich is actually
a Catholic, and the press never forgets to mention this fact, thus
inadvertently helping to consolidate the image the Roundtable
coalition would like to have. Interestingly enough, there are no
signs as yet that Weyrich has ever clashed with the hierarchy
of the Roman Catholic Church.

Obviously, Weyrich rides from morality to politics on the vehicle of abortion, which he uses to obtain support or at least
benevolence from the Catholic Church, just as the Moral Majority uses the issue of Zionism to maintain its image of respec-
tabliity in the eyes of non-Christian conservatives. These two
immensely important issues, with their endless capacity for mass
mobilization, would provide reason enough to doubt Lipset and
Raab's claim that the Christian Right is an irrelevant part of a

political change that should be defined in entirely different terms. According to the *Commentary* article, Christian conservatism is no more or less important than the John Birch Society, the extreme right-wing group that gained considerable notoriety in the sixties. When the press stopped reporting on that organization, say Lipset and Raab, it continued to exist, but in the eyes of the public it became irrelevant. They maintain the same could happen at any moment in the case of the Moral Majority.

Although they claim the Moral Majority is only one aspect of the new phenomenon and certainly not its most influential, the two social scientists decided to study it because they needed support for their minimalization of the issue. They chose to ignore the long-standing political clout of such Christian pressure groups as Weyrich's committee and the Religious Roundtable. Their article overlooked the great issues that these organizations support with the crazed frenzy of a religious crusade, such issues as abortion, creationism, school prayer, and sex education, all clearly capable of mass mobilization. And it avoided analyzing the techniques and modus operandi of these groups, which despite their alleged marginal nature seem able to seduce and thus politically inspire much larger forces, such as the Catholic Church through the abortion issue and part of the Jewish opinion through "Zionism." Finally, Lipset and Raab chose to ignore the novelty, which was that no United States President had ever before officially accepted the support of groups which appeared to be (as indeed the authors claim these are) politically and culturally out of sync. This certainly never happened in the case of the John Birch Society, of which the official conservative groups and prestigious leaders such as Senator Goldwater has always steered clear.

Yet this coalition of groups, which Lipset and Raab allege to be so small and uninfluential, has free access to the White House, it has realistic chances of influencing television programs, is in direct contact with Congress, and can seduce such forces as the Catholic and Jewish communities into collaboration with their plans.

We have seen how neo-Christian interference has led to polarization and the threat of fracture within the Catholic and Jewish communities. Fundamentalist Christianity seems able to fill the gap between the benevolent disapproval of *Commentary* and the outraged dissent of Pisar and Hertzberg; between passionate Catholic participation in the antiabortion campaign and that Church's doubts about the new administration's fiscal rigor, which many bishops define as "antipoor"; and clear policy differences with regard to the delicate balance between stability, rebellion, and right and left terrorism in Latin America. At any rate, the New Christian Right seems able to create unbalance in groups much larger than itself and then use that unbalance to its own advantage. It has accentuated subtle conflicts that have already provoked much greater consequences.

Paul Weyrich, the Catholic, tells the neo-Christians of the Religious Roundtable "not to worry about complaints of mixing religion and politics because liberal church people . . . have testified for every cuckoo social welfare program that comes down the path. Nor . . . should they worry about charges that people like me from the New Right were using Christians. Neither side is using the other, but they share beliefs that are important in the 'fight of values' going on in Washington" (*New York Times*, April 12, 1981). Thus the phenomenon may be a transitory one, but that does not make it any less important. Not only has it pushed other churches to espouse political positions in an unprecedented fashion, but in so doing it has split and thus weakened its own allies. What has been happening to the mainstream Protestant churches over the past few years is yet another indication that Lipset and Raab may have been too optimistic in their evaluations.

THE DANGER FOR MAINSTREAM PROTESTANTISM

In its studies of American religion, the Survey Research Center of the University of California usually compares the "liberal" churches (Episcopalian, Presbyterian, and Methodist) with the "fundamentalist" churches, using this term as a synonym for "conservative." Other surveys like Gallup and Harris list the mainstream churches on the one hand, including Presbyterians, Methodists, Unitarians, and Lutherans, and a generic group of "evangelicals" on the other. The Church of Jesus Christ of the Latter-day Saints is not included in these statistics, but not because it is irrelevant. On the contrary, it is an extremely important sect, but it is eliminated because it is a powerful but local church confined almost entirely to the two states where it originated, Utah and Missouri.

No matter which churches are included in these two large groupings, with one being more liberal and the other dedicated to rigor and the conservation of the past, it is hard to conceal the way the mainstream churches have been losing 1 percent of their worshipers each year while the fundamentalists have been steadily gaining 2 percent. To have an idea of the size of these figures, one would have to consider that they refer to over 40 percent of the adult population of the country. However, the numbers do not say much, or at least not everything, about the evolution of American religious belief within the mainstream churches themselves. Those who tend to play down the strength of neo-Christian conservatism point to the fact that most statistical surveys include the Baptist churches under the "evangelicals" heading, even though seven out of thirteen millions of Baptist churches are black, therefore their perception of present-day reality is probably different from the one of white Baptist churchgoers. What is more, even the evangelical movement itself is aware that it is subdivided into two hazily defined but significant camps with regard to inter- and intragroup relations. The first is represented by the periodical *Christianity Today* and has its most popular spokesman in Billy Graham. This is the moderate wing of the formation. The other camp's newspaper is the *Christian Voice*. Led by Jerry Falwell, leader of the Moral Majority, it is the bastion of spiritual, religious, and political neo-conservatism in America.

These subdivisions give us an idea of the political clout of conservative Christianity. Certainly it cannot outweigh the energy of the Baptist and evangelical churches, groups, and movements, which have no political affiliation. But it is just as definitely the strongest form of Christian conservatism that has ever existed in the history of American Protestantism in the postwar decades. On the other hand, if we abandon the usual map of theological and dogmatic boundary lines, we will quickly see that there are three vast religious regions in America. The first includes the mainstream and liberal churches, but it also includes the evangelicals and Baptists represented by *Christianity Today* and Billy Graham. The second area is black religion. The third is neo-evangelical fundamentalism, also called neo-Christianity or the New Christian Right, which espouses all the strongly conservative positions mentioned previously.

The relationship between religious events and political facts shows that this third group is currently going through a stage of great dynamism. It can create audacious new alliances, interfere dramatically with public activity, and act imaginatively upon the establishment churches. Recently, the National Council of Churches, which represents most large Protestant churches of America, has been on the defense under bitter ideological attack accused of being too liberal and harboring a "Third-World"-type of cultural judgment over international issues.

In religious terms, the controversy that has split American evangelicalism into Billy Graham and Jerry Falwell camps can be defined as "modernism vs. fundamentalism." This means that the fundamentalists' literal belief in the infallible truth of the Bible opposes the modernists' open and critical interpretation influenced by culture and history. The fragmentary structure of Protestantism makes it impossible to use these terms to evaluate the social and political strength of the different movements. Fundamentalism itself abounds with signs of opposition to the sharp rightward swerve its leaders have taken, and the present phase might easily be followed by an entirely different one. Furthermore, this view of the situation takes no account of the role played by black religion. Almost all of the black Baptist

churches are theologically aligned on the side of fundamentalism against modernism. But when the white wing of the religious conservative movement calls them to political action, few
blacks respond. Although fundamentalists carefully calculate the
presence of at least one black pastor at every public event, the
various forms of conservative Christianity have yet to produce
even one second-echelon black leader. Thus it must be considered that millions of the worshippers who can be counted
among the antimodernist ranks from the theological point of view
are nonetheless unwilling to participate in right-wing political
commitment.

At any rate, it is all a question of stages, and each stage is
dominated by a handful of people. Within Catholicism, a pope
determined to unify his Church has opened the way for the
faithful to participate in crusades whose extreme nature and
whose political consequences create internal unbalance. As we
have seen, this all occurred because the neo-evangelicals and
John Paul II both radicalized their stands on abortion at almost
the same moment in time and with almost the same words.
Within Jewish culture, the convergence, albeit temporary, of
the political position of one party (the Likud) with the definition of the "centrality of Israel" has sensitized broad moderate
masses to the apparent equivalence between Israel as the purpose of Zionism and Israel as the political strategy of Likud. Thus
once again a "coincidental" convergence has been intelligently
exploited by the New Christian Right, particularly by the fundamentalist and evangelical groups for whom relations with
Jewish culture would otherwise have appeared to be impossible.

Thus we are dealing with a very dynamic political and religious minority which has been extremely receptive to the fa-
vorable climate of the times, duly pragmatic in its relations with
the other part of evangelicalism, and flexible in its at least temporary alliances with Catholics and Jews. At the same time, it
has been ruthless, aggressive, and derisive with regard to the
"liberal churches," as we have seen in the worlds of Paul Weyrich
and the Religious Roundtable.

Simultaneously, those liberal churches have been facing a delicate season of redefinition of goals and priorities. Today mainstream Protestantism is paying the price for the wide hospitality it accorded to the new proposals and cultural programs of the sixties and seventies. Meanwhile, the evangelicals have flooded America with fundamentalist Bibles, the most famous of which is a Nashville-published Thomas Nelson edition, with twenty-two million copies now in circulation.

The Council of Churches has seemed to be preocupied and uncertain with respect to the antimodernist coalitions created by neo-Christianity. It is natural for a highly sophisticated intellectually oriented body to be aware of the many religious and secular implications of any move. But for now we are left with the prospect of a time of prosperity for the New Christian Right. Although this front controls only a small part of the country's religious belief, it has formed unprecedented allegiances and bonds. In so doing, it has shown tremendous courage, and it has anticipated all the other religious cultures in America. In this sense, the right-wing movement is first of all the achievement of an audacious "right-wing church," which is the most visible force behind all the organizational and political planning, legislative reform, and group movements in the new conservative America of the eighties.

FIVE

Faith, Secrets, and Conspiracy

In the United States, every bona fide church organization is entitled to complete tax-exempt status on all its property and profits. Whenever there is dispute about that privilege, the issue at stake is never the nature or content of the church. What the courts try to investigate is the intricate and often confounding distinction between strictly religious activities—regardless of the cult's objectives or tenets—and other activities, particularly in political or economic terms.

For more than three years, the Unification Church, popularly known as "the Moonies," after its Korean founder and charismatic leader, the Reverend Sun Myung Moon, fiercely defended itself against allegations that it was more a political force than a religious organization. Moon managed to exhibit Catholic, Protestant, and Jewish testimony to the exclusively religious character of his new church, and he even had the omnipresent American Civil Liberties Union defend his sect. Nevertheless, in 1982 the Court of Appeals of the State of New York decided, with only one dissenting vote, that the Unification Church uses its organization and facilities to promote activities that should be defined as political or business oriented rather than religious and that therefore the church is not eligible to receive the tax-exempt status normally accorded to organizations with spiritual goals.

This ruling did not break or even weaken the single most powerful religious organization that has appeared in the United States over the past twenty years. But the investigation and media coverage of federal allegations and "Moonie" defense shed some light on the way the movement had formed and expanded. As a consequence it became easier to understand the whole phenomenon of organized religion in comtemporary America.

In its four hundred years of existence, America has gone through an initial phase of spiritual consolidation and several successive waves of intense change, renewal, proliferation, and fracture. There was the Second Awakening before the Civil War; in the 1930s, the fervor of the evangelical preachers and charismatic movements was a response to the economic collapse of the Depression. Not many attempts have ever been made to study the correlation between socioeconomic conditions and the appearance or disappearance of religious movements. Yet there is no doubt that each great season of fracture and formation has corresponded to times of political transition, economic crisis or uncertainty, sweeping social change, and radical cultural modification. For instance, as the Second Awakening rolled westward with the settlers, it marked—or at least proclaimed the arrival of—the end of Northeastern cultural dominance over the South and West. This was when the Lutheran church split into two synods; it was when the Mormon church, destined itself to crack into the Utah and Missouri congregations, was founded; and it was when the Church of Christ, Scientist, began. During the same period, several evangelical and fundamentalist groups started their own independent sects, which later joined to form larger denominations.

Between the two world wars and especially during the thirties, widespread precariousness created optimal conditions for evangelical preachers, with their faith in direct salvation and the miracle. Later, the sixties counterculture gave a sharp jolt to the whole political and cultural establishment, and the shock was felt by the churches as well. The revolt and protest were short-lived, but they occurred in a society that tends to express its tensions by creating new churches rather than by consolidating new political parties, and so the consequent religious reawakening has affected the entire two decades from the sixties to the eighties.

DEFENSE BY SECRECY

Most probably, the typical signs of the new culture will be transitory, suited as they are to the trauma of new settlements. The sects that do last are destined to evolve into a new generation of respectable establishment religions. In the meantime, however, there is no doubt that this renewed religious vitality has already spawned new precedents. First, there is the political aspect: whether they are "right-wing" or "leftist," the birth of these sects is always related to such nonreligious features as political conservatism, Marxism, or Third World ideology. In addition, their very structure is a novelty, with its tendency toward secrecy and self-segregation, proselytism even to the point of abduction, and conspiratory aura.

These traits, which typify such leftist churches as Jonestown or the Christian World Liberation Front, are just as prevalent in such right-wing cults as the Unification Church, the Universal Church of God, or the Children of God. But they can also be found in groups that practice strict political abstention, such as Hare Krishna and the Divine Light Mission. Even the semireligious cults and psychological training programs of est have seen the usefulness in certain elements of secrecy, and this decision may have contributed to the success they have had for over a decade.

The Court of Appeals ruling on the Unification Church (and the final Superior Court confirmation of the verdict) was significant, because it showed the discomfort of American culture with regard to the new religious denominations and their tendency to avoid the public eye and consider any outside attention a form of persecution. But what has created these secrecy cults? What aspects of social life and custom have led to such radical spiritual and political choices? Why has each of these groups adopted the same basic charismatic style, personalization and veneration of the leader, deprivation of the believer's personality and identity, exasperation of the acts of faith, exaltation of the miracle, and disinterest in harmonizing with anything "external" or social? And finally, why is it that anything outside the cult is experienced as a hostile conspiracy against which the followers feel obliged to defend themselves, or perhaps even to attack in advance?

All of these characteristics are typical of the new American cults born over the last two decades. New American religions have not always been typified this way. Today's sects have their own peculiar set of sociological motivations, inasmuch as all the "conspiracy" cults, from the lowest and most abhorrent Manson family to the strongest and most organized Synanon, have all come in some way from the sixties counterculture. And there is the common political background. Moreover, the aggressive desire to conquer that compensates for a sense of persecution has not remained an exclusive feature of the obscure cults that grew out of the sixties. Now it has been transplanted to the conservative fundamentalist and evangelical Christianity that is the political mainstay of the eighties. Two clear examples of this attitude come to mind: the censorship campaign to eliminate school textbooks considered "humanistic" because they are not strictly Christian, and the obstinate neo-Christian habit of defining the world according to its own indisputable and absolute criteria of "right" and "wrong."

IS THE CHURCH-STATE SEPARATION COMING TO AN END?

The most important aspect of the "revolutionary" events sparked by America's new religions and the primary innovation in the organizational forms those religions have established for themselves is the relationship with political institutions, which may oscillate among escape, antagonism, fear, self-segregation, and militancy, but has never been one of indifference or respectful distance. Throughout the adventures of American spirituality, no matter how America's new cults had been organized, both sides—church and state—had always maintained the secular principle of church-state separation. In all the centuries of America's existence, more than in any other Western country, the institutions have called upon God and religion, while the churches have made themselves into schools of moral discipline and civil obedience.

Of course there have been noteworthy exceptions, such as the illegal polygamy of the Mormons and some states' delay or unwillingness to give equal rights to the Jewish, Catholic, and black churches. But every one of these instances has found its resolution in the principle of separation. The Mormons have accepted federal law without changing the teachings of the church, merely keeping them from exceeding the limits of peaceful coexistence. After long periods of dramatic conflict, Catholics, Jews, and blacks have acquired judicial equality and social acceptance. Certain times and governments have been besieged by religious fervor or surrounded by religious indifference, but the basis for relations has always been separation. If this foundation has survived at all, it is thanks to the shared belief that an impartial state is presiding on the bench, considering and balancing everyone's needs and demands.

Ideology has appeared only sporadically on the American cultural and political scenes, but its explosions have left permanent scars. During the Sacco and Vanzetti crisis, the Catholic church was forced to restore discipline among Italian masses when immigrant anarchists clashed with the establishment.

In the sixties, it was the black pastors of the American South, working in moral solidarity with the National Council of Churches and Jewish and Catholic leadership, who kept the battle for civil rights within limits of strict nonviolence. In all instances, America's federal institutions acted in reply. The New Deal was a response to the frustrated hopes of the poor masses and each successive wave of immigrants. American intervention in World

War II transformed all antifascist and anti-Nazi militancy into a tidal wave of participation in the American ideal. Later, under the guidance of such presidents as Kennedy and Johnson, the American Congress gave angry black masses an adequate legislative response to the demands that their religious leaders had presented.

Thus things progressed in relatively harmonious fashion. The federal government never had to legislate moral persuasions, and it established broad limits of tolerance for every faith. On the other hand, it never failed to act every time there was a need to protect a cult. So governments, too, were able to comply with the messages of the churches while respecting church-state separation. It is in the name of this separation that the United States only recently sent an ambassador to the Holy See, even though the Catholic religion, with its fifty million American followers, is the most powerful spiritual organization in the country.

But something changed during the sixties. The violence of such phenomena as the Black Panthers, African nationalism, the Weathermen, and the Symbionese Liberation Front was short-lived, but the effects of anti-Vietnam oppsition have lingered. Although it was not led by the churches, this was nevertheless the first time that a revolt against the institutions had been motivated more by moral protest than by ideology. Its nature was clearly political, even though for the most part it took place outside the parties and well away from the effective range of the institutions. The widespread feeling of opposition to and alienation from every form of power created cultural and psychological distance, diversity, and diffidence for the first time in relations between voluntary groups and American federal institutions. Certainly such a situation had never occurred before in this century.

What happened next is common knowledge. The establishment churches somehow managed to regain their function of leadership, but not without negotiation and adjustment. So in America, the Catholic Church gained new social militancy and the National Council of Churches gravitated leftward. At the same time, the political institutions suffered the rites of purification with Watergate and thus were able to retrieve their credibility and return to center stage. Nonetheless, a widespread feeling of alienation has remained, and this gap has been filled by the new cults, which have formed ranks first to the left and then to the right of the traditional middle ground where political power and religious institutions have always coexisted.

PROSELYTISM, INTOLERANCE, AND PERSECUTION

From its very inception, this new generation of militants has shared a dream of usurping the right to establish absolute definitions of "right" and "wrong." In addition, they have tended to disregard the traditional role of the state, or at least to distrust it, shun it, challenge it, and even attempt to subvert it. For the first time, these new religious conglomerations have not defended the doctrine of tolerance. On the contrary, they have established a set of conditions, drawn out a territory of exclusive rights, or called for a challenge to the state laws. This phenomenon has had three easily identifiable mechanisms: passionate, boundless missionary fervor; isolation and fear of persecution; and the tendency to create pressure groups hell-bent upon shaping legislation and government to the demands of new truths conceptualized in the bosom of the church.

The first mechanism belongs to the multitude of sects rooted in the Jesus movement and Eastern religions. The second distinguishes such groups as the Christian World Liberation Front, the People's Temple, and a horde of tiny paranoid, arrogant, isolated sects with a penchant for creating parallel or separate social orders. The third seems to show up above all in the evangelical and fundamentalist cults. Although these are no novelty in American spirituality, they have a new way of nominating themselves to be political counterparts whose goals are to challenge, condition, and possibly even control the state. What we are seeing here might be defined as an end to church-state separation, or at least a full-fledged attempt to end it. This occurs when a cult ignores or even repudiates the state, or when it intends to bend the nation's laws to its vision.

The American Constitution charters an inflexible separation between civil and religious communities, at the same time that they establish an almost complete correspondence of values, goals, and ideals. Today's conditions of antagonism and friction involve only certain sectors of American religious culture, which are embodied in the cults born or "refounded" after the anti-state experience of the sixties. While the motivations behind these cults may seem to differ, contrast, or even oppose one another, all these neophyte groups possess the same aura of challenge, which it seems can no longer be expressed within the traditional cooperation-separation way of existing. Some manifestations of this detachment, such as the Jesus Children movement, have been short but intense; others, such as the sects inspired by Eastern religion or philosophy, have represented cultural exile with no return, although the number of their disciples and the impact of their social consequences have been limited. Still others, like the People's Temple, have burned themselves out in bitterness, conflict, and tragedy.

In the meantime, however, a whole group of cultural aggregations that seemed to have been born on the left was now regrouping and revitalizing on the right. Their new challenge is every bit as vehement as previous revolts, but this time the organization is far more coherent and its proposals are far more solid. The new fundamentalism does not call for a return to the common goals of church and state, much less a return to mutual respect based on separation. It has every intention of imposing the superiority of religious tenets over political principles, and it is determined to enforce religion's prerogative to redefine what the law considers "right" and "wrong."

The new cultists have cultural reasons for their move from left to right. The birth of the self-culture, self-help, and self-development eras has brought the urge to save oneself before anything else; simultaneously, a wide range of training programs, philosophies, and practical or theoretical positions have helped to banish the traditional sentiments of compassion and solidarity and invalidate the common view of history. There have been political reasons, as a widespread redistribution of opinion has created a conservative front. And there have been economic factors, as the passage from growth to crisis in the seventies has caused fear and confusion among the middle-class whites who make up the most influential faction of the new religious militancy.

EXODUS: FROM THE CHURCHES TO THE CULTS

One example that might be examined as a model for the new type of religion is the Christian World Liberation Front. As ephemeral as it is widespread, the front began in Berkeley toward the end of the sixties. By 1971, it had gained enough notoriety to warrant cover stories in both *Time* and *Newsweek*. Like most of the Jesus cults that spread from California through the rest of the United States, like the Eastern cults, and like most of the radical political groups that dominated during those years, the front was founded upon belief in the end of the world. Theirs was not a physical doomsday: it was the projected demise of a culture and a philosophy, an end to the organizations and institutions of the world as they existed then.

The consequences of this type of millenarianism most often surface in disapproval, disdain, and detachment from everything having anything to do with officially accredited culture: the universities, the mainstream churches, family- and church-inspired rules of behavior, tolerance in interpersonal relations. There is an overall need to discredit and violate, and while there is also a desire to disobey, it is less pressing than the firm determination to obey a different set of rules that are thought to be superior to current values. If necessary, this difference and superiority may be applied not only to legislation but also to the institutions that make and enforce those laws, as well as to the organs of authority and its traditional representatives, the family and the schools.

This attitude does not necessarily have to erupt into subversive, antagonistic, or revolutionary behavior. Jim Jones and his followers have been the only relevant examples of active, deliberate violation. In most cases, these different and superior new values materialize mainly in the form of resistance. But what may easily occur is that this resistance evolves into persecution mania. Most of the time such groups voluntarily adopt a conspiratory or semisecretive attitude, which can easily be used as a means of defense and a guarantee of purity. This is where the old religions leave off and the new ones begin.

Before we go on to identify the many kinds of radicalism, extremism, or religious militancy that have been proposed by the new cults and sects, we should first point out that everything which has come out of the sixties counterculture has borne the stamp of fracture and a penchant for "resistance." This may quickly change into attack, secrecy, or disapproval of common values, particularly of those "exalted" values dear to the academic institutions and to the cultural establishment. Every one of these cults sees itself as a potential counterpart of the state. When there is no real basis for power and consensus, as in the Jonestown incident, the challenge collapses or leads to tragedy. When that challenge is realistically possible, it takes the form of peremptory edicts, which present the political or social powers with the alternatives of surrender or siege. This is what has happened on the issue of abortion, with the Moral Majority demanding absolute prohibition no matter what the religious or other circumstances. And it is what occurred when the same groups began their campaign against the American television networks, in an effort to blackball programs they felt did not fit the requirements established by their absolute criteria for what is "right." The same mechanism has fueled repeated crusades for the censorship of books, which are occasionally burned in macabre public bonfires.

But let us go back to the origins of something that might be defined as a huge faultline crossing the psychological and cultural landscape of America, of which religion is only one aspect. And let us see how initial rumblings along this faultline have upset the clear-cut distinction between what political jargon would call "right-wing" and "leftist" tendencies.

IN SEARCH OF JESUS: THE "EXPERIENCE," SALVATION, AND THE MIRACLE

In a National Council of Churches report on the birth of the new leftist Christian sects, Donald Heinz of Berkeley's Graduate Theological Union describes one—if not the—germinal point of the new religions.

Toward the end of the Sixties, a new historical definition of Jesus began to take shape. The so-called "youth culture" greatly resembled the stereotypes of the times: flower children, hippies, teenagers enchanted by drugs, disappointed radicals, children fleeing from overly permissive families and from churches whose teachings were insipid and banal. This culture had been called "a sign of capitalist decadence" by the Marxists, "future shock" by Alvin Toffler, "a counterculture that was generating itself" by Theodore Roszak, "an irreparable fracture of American culture" by Philip Slater, "the beginning of an American rejuvenation" by Charles Reich, "a protean state" by Robert Jay Lifton, and "a hopeless one-way trip" by Robert Bellah. What caused the most disorientation was profound uncertainty about morality and lifestyles. Technology gave a sense of antagonism and itself became a scapegoat. Astrology, the occult, magic, the movement for "the development of human potential" and the Eastern religions all became an attractive way out, not to mention drugs and regression to childhood. One of the answers, found by a great many youths, was the name, symbol and figure of Jesus. . . . So the emergence of the figure and attraction of Jesus became the focal point of the religions experience of the Late Sixties. An experience so widespread that it could truly be called a "Jesus movement."

Out of this movement came a group of fairly young people, almost all of whom had actively participated in the search for political solutions. The group went on to form the Christian World Liberation Front, whose name alone immediately reveals its radical leftist origins. But as the many studies and sociological surveys of the phenomenon have shown, what really determined the group's choices and collaboration was the choice of Jesus as the alternative to politics, social commitment, militancy, drugs, previous personal life-styles, family mores, and the lack of religion or regular worship. It is to these situations that the sect members themselves claim to have reacted. When Jesus is conceived as an alternative, He can easily be used to justify the abandonment, distrust, disinterest, and challenge of everything that does not totally coincide with that alternative. This means abandonment not only of the politics of opposition, but also of the other debate partner: the cultural establishment. Once seen as an omnipresent enemy, it is now as remote and irrelevant as the causes for which the movement once fought. Along with the sense of the alternative, these groups also exalt the concepts of "salvation" and "experience" dear to the other Jesus cults. To say "only Jesus is salvation" is to passionately and energetically reject history. In fact the new Jesus can only save when there is complete oneness with Him, and His salvation does not require any sort of action, except for total and absolute belief in Him. The Catholic doctrine and the prevalent Protestant attitude about salvation through faith *and* charitable works are wiped out. Thus, despite the mellowness that has permeated the Jesus movement, the fundamental value of charity has been eliminated, and with it has gone the Christian sense of social action.

As numbers of new converts have slithered along a path that secular terminology would describe as going from left to right, this aspect has been radically important. Any call for the social and compassionate component of Christian faith has withered away, replaced by a sense of "instant salvation" or a state of grace that can only be maintained through what is thought to be an intimate, total, and all-inclusive relationship with Jesus, which eventually leads to complete oneness with Him. The mental state that ensues has no room for social or public acts, just as it makes culture and learning pointless. Thus a fixed ideal thought to be incapable of mutation replaces the adventure of exploration, the will to know, and the need to acquire and confront experiences. And despite all the mellowness, the fact that this outlook requires no verification through confrontation with hard facts and reality means it inevitably acquires rigidity, spurns social relations and compromise, and breeds intolerance, even if the mass of neophyte believers does not consider it so.

Absolute faith in salvation through oneness with Jesus goes hand-in-hand with another part of the preaching found in all the Jesus cults: the "experience." Anyone familiar with these movements in the United States in recent years knows the expression, "to experience Jesus," the obsessive mantra repeated ad nauseum by so many former protagonists of the counterculture turned religious leaders. This outlook has pushed the Jesus movement even farther from traditional reasoning and closer to a rigid ascetic search for the miracle. Countless theology, sociology, and psychology departments of America's universities are brimming with data on the new phenomenon of "experiencing" Jesus, the historical connotations of which implied a deeper and more intimate knowledge of Jesus and His teachings, subsequent to a traditional conversion. But this concept was soon overthrown in favor of instant transformation, which brought the movement even closer to the charismatic and pentecostal cults.

The loudly proclaimed change that followed the Jesus "experience," which was usually "indescribable," could only reinforce the sense of alienation from people and institutions that had not undergone that experience. As a consequence, the group or movement would draw in around a few elements of absolute faith, and this would eventually lead to a break with the social environment, fear of anything on the outside, rigid enforcement of personal discipline, and intolerance of others. From this point on, any sense of social proportion or church-state, culture-religion, science-faith relations vanished or lost its purpose. Neo-Christianity has no room for the old "Render unto Caesar the things which are Caesar's" attitude, and it has unknowingly repressed most of Christianity's complex theological doctrine, replacing it with the figure, image, and charisma of Jesus as the exclusive overwhelming nucleus of faith. In disqualifying the theological underpinnings of Christian teachings, neo-Christianity has established a heretical beachhead on a remote island well away from the currents of mainstream Christian and secular culture.

It is hard to understand how the leaders of American Protestantism failed to notice the transformation that was occurring in relations between religious and lay spheres. Such publications as *The Christian Century* and pulpit celebrities as Billy Graham, destined twenty years later to become the staunch adversaries of fundamentalist Christianity and conservative evangelicalism, never noticed the original distortion; indeed, they welcomed the movement wholeheartedly, perhaps because they were overjoyed to be witnessing the end of the political counterculture. "The movement" had gone religious, and as such it was thought to be "good" or at least "better." "A bright seed in a sad wasteland, the veil that has been removed from the boredom of traditional religious conservatism and liberalism, a new sense of authority and love, in this simple and innocent cry of youth." These were the poetic words of Billy Graham, who failed to add that those "innocent" youths were also busy creating a new intolerance of which he would soon become a target.

PERSECUTION MANIA AND THE EUPHORIA OF
DOMINANCE

To these basic features, the "alternative," the "salvation," and the "experience," we should add another, and that is the apocalyptical element inherent in the imminent return of the Messiah. It was this belief that begot the flourishing branch of Christianity known as Jews for Jesus, But above all, this belief—which was every bit as passionate, absolute, and rigid as the others—introduced the element of doomsday as justification for the urgent and peremptory nature of the movement's demands upon the state, legislators, the judicial system, teachers, and the family: in other words, everything that is not organized religion. And it paved the way for two new forms of social organization: the conspiratory church and rigorous cultural and psychological isolation. These tendencies have erupted into grim atrocities ranging from Jonestown to Synanon. The combination of apocalyptic beliefs and charismatic cult in the neo-Christian movement eventually produce the euphoria of dominance, an ecstasy that is blind to the significance of church-state separation and to the wisdom of "giving in" to moderation. And so the chain of fundamentalist and evangelical aggregations has gained yet another link. All these groups refuse to acknowledge any historical background for their cults. Charity has been cut off from faith. Faith calls for actions related only to faith. Faith will not allow itself to be measured by history.

This is no new occurrence in Christianity or in American religion, but it is a debut in the heart of an industrial democracy. The self culture has also blossomed during the same years, profoundly changing American culture with its secular march toward the same isolation from social and political life and its establishment of a new brand of conservatism, based less upon political choice than a different outlook vis-à-vis social activities. With its new perspective, the secular self culture actually reinforces and extends the effects and maneuverability of the new religions. The tenets of those religions may be unknown to the self culture, and the two may not even be aware of the de facto alliance which they have implicitly formed. Nevertheless, like the new fundamentalist religions, the self culture places the individual, and the individual alone, mindless of the social environment, at the center of life's experiences, fantasies, and desires. But just what kind of self is this culture proposing? It is the individual, to be sure. But it is not individual meant to be free and exalted and celebrated as such in the Ayn Rand tradition. If this were the case, the self culture would only be one more repetition of American history, harking back at least as far as de Tocqueville's day.

THE COMMANDMENTS OF THE SELF CULTURE

In this new version, the self is *a* private individual, someone who cannot be measured against any other being, value, aggregation, or individual. This self comes first; it takes first place and resides in the very center of things. Novelty irritates it because new things have nothing to do with it. Newspapers and public activities irritate it. But this is no case of introversion, shyness, or withdrawal. It is a matter of sociology, not psychology. And it is an entirely original matter, at that. After the great frontier adventures of the individual, America lived through decades of social solidarity and community life. Finally, toward the end of the sixties, a new type of individual was born, delivered by the new schools of psychology, nurtured by Eastern philosophy and its techniques, and raised by the new and lucrative training centers and self-discovery institutes. This new model knows how to use every available instrument, resource, energy, and practical or cultural technique for the exclusive purpose of "self-fulfillment." And here the definition of the self culture's individual concludes. This culture never mentions whether other selves will benefit from the improvement of one self. No one ever claims that a society of individuals who can accept and fulfill each separate personal self is a better society. There are simply no references made to the "rest" of the self culture.

Of course, this culture does not advise blindness or ignorance; its frank recommendation is for indifference. This attitude, which is for instance the very fundament of the est training program, can have obvious therapeutic purposes, considering the anguish of today's individuals in the face of the unresolvable problems of the world, the nation, the group, the worksite, and even the family. Self-fulfillment tends to create euphoria, which comes from the feeling of unburdening oneself of a heavy load (the "burden of history" or the "burden of others") and from the conviction that one has nothing to do with the political, social, and economic problems afflicting the world. This euphoria is very similar to the type of elation felt by the Pentecostalists, the charismatic cults, and the new-Christians when they "experience" Jesus, God, or the Holy Ghost. The mystic quality of the religious experience distinguishes it from the secular one, but both share the same detachment from the world, and it unites them in an unspoken bond of sympathy.

This may be another reason for the enormous success of the conservative GOP in the 1980 elections, when the call for "less government" or even more drastic demands to "get the government off our backs, out of our lives, and out of our business" seemed to strike an almost universal chord. Many opinion surveys have taken the wrong approach in judging this phenomenon. The change was not brought about by political mood or ideological choice alone. It was also caused by a new counterculture that rose from the ashes of the King and Kennedy assassinations, the Vietnam debacle, and the Watergate disgrace, all of which had combined to convince many Americans that their country was on the brink of collapse.

Thus like the radical counterculture and neo-Christianity, the self culture owes its vigor to an outlook that views the world as a terminal patient. Because this perspective is so apocalyptical, it is more than compatible with religious fundamentalism. It leads to total disbelief in salvation by other mortal entities, be they institutions, international organizations, or governments, and it germinates the "save yourself first" attitude, which blossoms into the determination to set out on a new course or to dedicate one's life to obstinate self-improvement. Or it leads to the equally individual "experience of God," with its alienation from those who have not had the same experience and its inducement to fear anything different.

This kind of psychological and cultural viewpoint has only contempt for the uncertainty, ambivalence, and mutability of history. Once again, the self culture and the new religions have lined up on the same side of the battlefield. The threats of history (upon which Europe still relies obsessively for its culture and rules of conduct, and is thus even further alienated from America) can only be defeated by something immovable and indisputable, something that is strong enough to put an end to undesirable debate about all those unbearable alternatives. This something might be the resounding cry for patriotism in the name of God. By combining the two the symbol can be glorified, even though it may not match the nation's actual laws and institutions. The need for this something justifies stubborn rejection of such international institutions as the United Nations, UNESCO, and FAO, not because of the objective deterioration of those institutions but due to the feeling that they are instruments of interference in a "pure" insular America. No such interference must be tolerated, because it introduces alien ideology, and also because the self culture and neo-Christianity both teach that the problems of the world are self-inflicted and pose a real threat to the certainties these groups have fought to acquire.

Thus what unites the secular self culture with neo-Christianity is the solution-by-repression technique. One example of this mechanism is the recent fundamentalist campaign to eliminate "doubt" from secondary school teaching. According to the plan, students are forbidden to express their own opinions, because these might easily differ from the simple and absolute values of "right" and "wrong." Teachers are told to eliminate ambivalence, doubt, and hypothetical thinking from their instruction. Records have shown that this tree of uncertainty can be defoliated only by brutal pruning, which leaves only naked, sure "truths." But this can now take place almost unhampered, because the self culture has no reason to disturb the militancy of absolute religion. Like fundamentalism, the self needs "social silence." Of course, this does not explain the broader and much more complex set of circumstances that transported America from the liberalism of Kennedy and Johnson to the pragmatism of Nixon and Ford, on to the uncertain internationalism of Carter, and finally to the conservatism of the eighties. Still, awareness of these parallel cultures can shed some light on the breadth and resonance of a situation that has reached far beyond the limits of normal political activity.

SURVIVALISM REINFORCES THE NEW RELIGIONS

Secrecy, conspiracy, and intolerance are always directly proportionate to a group's strength. As fear of outside danger grows,
the defense mechanisms of secrecy and conspiracy must be
strengthened and the weapons used in defense or offense must
be beefed up. Recent American religious history has been strewn
with ritual crimes and claims of persecution, as reporters have
revealed the beliefs or financial resources of such new cults as
the Unification Church. Endless court cases have been kept alive
to serve as defense barriers against intruders and investigations; families have kidnapped their own children to rescue them
fom the "imprisonment" of various cults; the same cults have
"counterkidnapped" or secluded their followers to "protect"
them. One instance of extremism was the poisonous snake which
Synanon disciples placed in the letter box of a lawyer who had
just won an appeal against the sect in a Los Angeles court: the
snakebite left its victim in a coma for some time. Undoubtedly,
the apex of fanaticism was reached by the People's Temple in
its Guayana mass suicide.

A different kind of arrogance and intimidation, apparently able
to challenge the state and bend laws to its force, has now appeared in the neo-Christian coalition that calls itself the Moral
Majority. Is it right to mention a cult of madmen willing to
commit mass suicide in the same breath as a movement that
seems levelheaded, organized to the point of victory, and capable of giving real dimension to the role its beliefs call for?
Certainly no facts warrant such a comparison. Although it must
be remembered that no one discovered Jim Jones' madness until it was too late, that insanity may very well have been a result of the typical conspiratory secrecy and isolation found among
some new sects. But fundamentalist Christianity possesses all
the means to express itself, gain the power to dominate, and
win the favor of broad and authoritative sectors of public opinion.

And yet there are aspects in common. First, there is the

apocalyptic outlook of world that can only be redeemed through a radical variation of its rules. And then there is the problem—indeed, the obsession—of survival, something we have already encountered under the name of "survivalism." Of course, when we speak of "common" values, we are not implying similar behavioral patterns or analogous threats. What these new radical religions have in common is an intricate tangle of roots, from which they grow and branch out into an incredible number of hybrids.

When Jim Jones went to Guayana to found Jonestown, he was convinced that survival was impossible under the conditions established by the society in which his church had been born. Fundamentalist conservative Christianity has actively and loudly orchestrated the elimination of countless political figures, among them faithful associates of Carter, Kennedy, and King, and they have heedlessly labored to wipe out entire chapters of history, culture, and international policy. But their program envisions an in situ solution that makes it unnecessary to emigrate; their plan calls for dramatic change in order to survive in the face of situations thought otherwise to be intolerably dangerous. In other words, the survivalist jargon used by the new right-wing coalition is no less extreme than the language of the sixties leftist religions. What has changed is the way of acting upon those pronouncements.

Like the self culture, the survivalism that has set the tone for the eighties is split into secular and religious factions. With each wing reinforcing the other, the resulting situation may change the whole image of American public activity. Here again the same new characteristics clearly distinguish this trend from past ones. Survivalism is introverted, and it rejects solidarity, disdains charity, and ignores the salvation of those who do not belong to the group, organization, or church. It teaches that universal salvation, is impossible, because only those who work actively and prepare to achieve it will be saved. Secular survivalism is every bit as rigid as the neo-Christian religious variety: "grace" is earned individually and cannot be given to others.

Every time a new form of secular survivalism is unveiled, the "scandal" lies in its determination to deny others access to the fruits of cultist labors. Weapons serve to keep others out of "my" bomb shelter, dynamite to blow up bridges leading to "my" secured place in case of emergency. Food ought to be withheld from those who have not thought ahead and accumulated enough for themselves and their families.

Once the apocalyptic principles of the survivalist culture have been accepted, such rigid morality makes sense. After all, if the world is going to end, everything must be prepared for that event. This is perfectly compatible with the principles of instant, individual, indivisible, and noncommunicable salvation preached by charismatic Christianity; it corresponds to the sense of damnation and imminent persecution that led to the People's Temple flight; and it fits right in with the principles of traditional conservatism, which teaches that good comes only from one's individual labor and never from collective activity, and that the fruits of such labor must not be shared with others, no matter what the reason.

There is one area where fundamentalism and survivalism seem to go separate ways. Conservative fundamentalist doctrines deny the existence of history and attempt to stop it at an ideal point, from which nothing is allowed to evolve, because change is the evil. But the real world undergoes constant transformation, so in the end this teaching is an invitation to move backward. On the other hand, survivalism is soaked in history, but it is determined to ignore the past and is exclusively and obsessively oriented toward the future, where it sees war, conflict, famine, destruction, monetary collapse, death, and the breakdown of economic systems, agreements, and universal laws.

The fact is that this sense of history is only apparent. A closer look at the situation shows that this perspective is no different from the concept of hellfire and damnation. Like the antihistoric religions, survivalism is founded on the contrast between absolute "right" and "wrong." History is experienced as a threatening adventure that must be fended off by immediately preparing the necessary protection, which is pictured in the same way that fundamentalist religion presents it: nonnegotiable. Just as we have seen for fundamentalism, nothing is debatable in the survivalist vision of the world. When (and not if) its predictions come true, there will be no time for discussion.

So it is that these apparently dissimilar social and religious trends are actually living under the same roof, in a house so littered with terrifying signals that any outside information must be shut out, because it might be deceitful. In this world, the only way to protect oneself is by huddling within a small introverted circle whose strength is in its conspiratory secrecy and exclusion. One typical feature of survivalist movements is to stop looking for more disciples once a certain "indispensable" number has been reached. This ideal nucleus for survival can include men, women, and children, but it must not be enlarged now or in the future. In the same way, the neo-Christian fundamentalists seem to have little interest in converting the masses. What proselytism does occur is due to the natural purpose of any church to make converts. But this urge takes a back seat to fundamentalist political commitment, which expends greater energy to identify enemies than to search for new friends.

THE AMBASSADORS AND EMISSARIES OF THE NEW CHURCHES

Like the People's Temple, the new fundamentalists do not maintain direct relations with the world of politics. The church comes to its own decisions and then expresses them through the mouths of chosen representatives, who may be loyal followers working "on the outside." These "ambassadors" and "allies" presumed to protect and advance the aims of the church are not required to obey the same rules dictated to the other disciples, because those are internal regulations which generally are not even publicized. From the very beginning, the Moral Majority made it clear that it had no intention of censoring, judging, or otherwise interfering in the private lives of senators and congressmen, as long as they were clearly willing to vote every time for the laws and measures supported and proposed by the religious coalition.

Allies of the infamous Jim Jones Temple were not necessarily believers, either. They were people who were willing to voice the charismatic message outside the church. For instance, this was the role played by Mark Lane, the lawyer who for a time supported and assisted Jim Jones. When Democratic Congressman Leo Ryan went to Guayana to investigate the situation, he was branded an enemy by the temple before he had officially expressed an opinion on the cult. By then the church had reached pathological levels of isolation and paranoia, and at that point the tension exploded into tragedy.

Other cults and churches of radically different brands of religious and political orientation seem to follow the same rules of conduct, although they do not carry them to such extreme limits. We have seen how large segments of contemporary Christianity are affected by rejection of prevailing culture, which means everything that is official, approved, and recognized, from the intellectual realm to the academic and scientific worlds. As the new churches see it, there is no distinction between culture and politics, because those two worlds are united by their shared acceptance of history. In rejecting history, the churches inevitably make their organizations more rigid, conservative, and nonnegotiable, not only in terms of beliefs but even in the very definition that each church gives itself. The end results are the "natural" mechanisms of separation and secrecy possessed by almost every sect or church formed in America since the beginning of the sixties. But these organizations are aware of outside reality, and so they pick out structures or individuals with which to have relations. To a man as simplistic and tormented as Jim Jones, someone like Mark Lane, trusted ally in a faithless wasteland, along with a handful of lawyers and treasurers, seemed to offer sufficient protection.

The evangelical Christian coalition elaborates complex and efficient mechanisms for each new issue as it arises. These techniques may be direct mailing centers for political mobili-

zation, which has been one function of the Moral Majority. Or
they may limit their efforts to one specific issue, as in the case
of the Committee for the Survival of a Free Congress, whose
job is to remove from office political figures considered dangerous to the new church front. Or they may be pressure groups
or media-watchdog agencies, like the organization created at the
beginning of 1981 to prepare and perform the campaign against
"non-Christian" television programming. Or they may focus all
their resources on one social issue (abortion) or on one line of
belief (creationism). The churches have no intention of discussing the principles they are defending. And they certainly do not
intend to use those principles as weapons on the political battlefield. And although they may use offense tactics, these organs of external communication are always mobilized in defense of the movement. They are an expression of the cult's latent
but clearly visible paranoia and persecution mania.

Sun Myung Moon's Unification Church a well-known examples. Partly because of the uproar he has caused, Moon almost never appears publicly alongside other members of the neo-
Christian coalition, although he shares their political stances almost item for item. The "Moonies" (who have only come to
embrace this nickname after furious attempts to suppress it) own
industries; they invest in the most profitable markets; they produce and distribute extremely costly movies. But the Unification Church almost never acts directly or overtly. Various in-
termediaries, who are often not even connected with the religious
or organizational side of the church, buy, negotiate, and sell on
its behalf. Only after painstaking investigations of complicated
financial transactions can the church sometimes be uncovered
as the beneficiary of its own operations. When the Moonies pass
from investment to management and production, they can then
rely—as we have learned frequently in the courts—upon the
unremunerated collaboration of cultists recruited through
proselytism and indoctrinated into church discipline. The sect's
opponents say its control over its followers comes from forced
isolation and the teachings of persecution and outside danger.

The disciples of such churches, who actively perform political, organizational, or financial roles in every capacity in the cult's enterprises, seem convinced that they are dedicating their efforts to physical and spiritual salvation from imminent doom. They all have the same total distrust of the outside, and this is reconfirmation of the three basic neo-Christian characteristics: the apocalyptic perspective; the rejection of history; and the sense of persecution that justifies any defense mechanism and all secrecy. For the first time in the history of modern industrial democracy, a part of the nation's population seems to have been swept up in a viewpoint—embodied in a religious faith—that opposes its political institutions, rejects the intricacies of international relations, disdains academic culture, and ignores the common experience of history.

SIX

In Search of a
Neutral God

In its celebrated 1947 *Everson* vs. *the Board of Education of Ewing Township* ruling, the United States Supreme Court found that the First Amendment "requires the state to be neutral in its relations with groups of religious believers and nonbelievers." More and more, the neo-Christians of America have been quoting this ruling to support their allegations that the nation's judicial system in recent decades has moved away from religion and "irreligion has now become a religion." In their estimation, such a serious threat to American morality can also create worrisome social and political predicaments. In its 1961 *Torcaso* vs. *Watkins* case, the Supreme Court deliberated yet another confrontation between religion and liberty. This time, the Court ruled that state and federal authorities may not approve legislation implying acceptance of principles specific to any particular faith, which may contrast with those of different beliefs. The Court went on to say that not even the principle of the existence of God should be the inspiration of legislation, because this would violate the constitutional rights of nonbelievers.

Rulings such as these have often been expressed by American courts in periods of political and cultural liberalism, when priority was given to the First Amendment (freedom of speech, press, assembly, and petition; complete religious freedom; separation of church and state). But recently, such verdicts have become a favorite target of new religions out to prove that America has been desecrated and that this desecration has violated the convictions of more than a few restricted Christian groups. According to fundamentalists, the essence of America have been debased, and while it may be hard to define the "essence" of America in terms of history, this has nonetheless become the battle cry in the self-indulgent literature of outraged neoevangelicals.

In 1980, the neo-Christians were thoroughly incensed by a policy change at Princeton University, one of the most prestigious private universities in the United States. Like all the other Ivy League schools, Princeton has evolved from one of the many religious institutions founded in early Protestant America. The extent of this evolution was made clear by a trustees' job description for dean of the Chapel, according to which, "henceforth the Dean should be a person of deep religious faith but above all he or she must be personally gracious and open, and his or her own religious commitment must include sensitivity to the vulnerability of human finitude and the particularity and relativity of the views he or she espouses." In other words, Princeton wanted to make sure the dean of its Chapel would be a religious intellectual and not a preacher to intellectuals. The neo-Christian reaction was concerted and vehement. Finally, their favorite enemy, liberalism produced by intellectualism and opposed to religion, could be publicly accused of scandal.

When neo-Christianity established its alliance with political conservatism, it extended this aggressive atmosphere to the Senate, to the point that for a while it seemed to be perfectly normal for the nation's legislature to debate the moment of life's conception so that abortion can be criminalized; the suppression or at least limitation of the teaching of the evolution theory in public schools (already outlawed in some states); and the introduction of the much-disputed bill on organized prayer in public schools that although defeated in Congress in March 1984 has promptly been reworded for further discussion.

THE DEBATE OVER STATE NEUTRALITY

The aggressivity of neo-Christianity is by now widely recognized. But less is known about the platforms these groups hope to popularize, which can be summarized as follows:

1. The state has no right to remain neutral in matters of faith. Faith lies well within the range of the law, inasmuch as it founded and should continue to inspire it. Because they are both part of God's will, neither the state nor the law can be neutral, and thus both must be either the expression or violation of that will.
2. God is neutral. He is not a partisan for or against any side. It is sacrilegious to imagine a conservative God fighting a liberal God. God is above these things. It is the duty of man to choose to be God's enemy or servant. The service of God is part of moral non-negotiable duty. Opposition to God and His tenets is not a constitutional right. Opposition to God is opposition to the state, inasmuch as the state represents harmonious coexistence of subjects with the will of God.

The day may come when these two propositions will seem only marginal episodes in America's development. But today they pose delicate problems. First there are the cultural implications of relations between different religions and sects; then there are the political consequences implicit in relations between faith and liberty. And finally, there are the legal complications of deciding whether a legislative body should rule in the name of a particular religious tenet, merely because part of the population thinks that tenet is universal and eternal. Statistical evaluation of the groups that support these extreme religious and political positions shows they are neither the core of American thinking nor the nation's majority sentiment. Nevertheless, as the strands of politics and religion have interwoven to make the tapestry of modern America, they have left unprecedented flaws which ought to be discussed.

The two Supreme Court rulings that the new Christians found so provocative and unacceptable, as well as the Princeton job description the fundamentalists termed "scandalous," were mentioned in an essay by the historian Terry Eastland, the gist of which was as follows: No one can claim the founding fathers of America were nonbelievers. Indeed, they established their nation upon the foundation of Christianity, and thus the principle of church-state separation makes no sense. The organizational, philosophical, and historical essence of the United States is based upon a fundamental Protestant document, the Larger Catechism of the Westminster Confession, which defines the ethics of social relations and even goes on to use those relations to define capitalism. Eastland quotes the German theologian Philip Schaff's 1844 reference to the "reigning theology of the country" to show that there is no way to distinguish between religious spirit, tradition, and history in the United States.

As the great immigrant waves arrived at the end of the last century, Protestantism began to lose its place as the "reigning theology," but this was the deliberate design of intellectuals and not a result of conflicting beliefs. To be more precise, it was the plan of "intellectuals, politicians, bureaucrats and the educated classes." These groups were responsible for what Eastland considers the historically inappropriate accent that has been placed on the American Constitution's famous protection of the right to pursue happiness. To Eastland, that right is alien to the religious fiber of America; he calls it the "fruit of the Age of Enlightenment and not of the Bible." In any case, the focal point was and should still be God, who is above partisan viewpoints, historical opposition, and legal perspectives.

Eastland deplores a lack of "authority" (which he defines in relation to his religious outlook) in the universities and in every other aspect of American intellectual life. He reminds us that authority is founded upon "values" that come before anything else, and that no constituency should be allowed to define its *own* values (Eastland's italics). He goes on to say that "since the Declaration of Independence America has held its commitments to liberty and virtue in tension." In a good representation of American neo-Christianity, Eastland claims that the country's historical tradition placed the accent on virtue and limited liberty according to each separate circumstance. If the spotlight has been shifted to liberty, he is sure it was at the hands of liberals, who thereby changed the original "liberty-virtue" conflict to a "liberty-license" tandem.

In conclusion, Eastland claims neo-Christian leaders have the right to intervene in politics because they are Christians. He recalls that Martin Luther King, a minister, did not hesitate to dive into the political maelstrom. To Eastland, King's acts were a product of the "liberal hypocrisy" that had secularized religion. Thus he defends the right of the new Christians to interfere in political matters, inasmuch as the values they sustain transcend politics. On the other hand, King can be opposed, debated, and even rejected, as though he were a politician, because he spoke not in the name of Christian values but in favor of secular beliefs, adjustments, and compromises that belonged to a political underworld.

DOES GOD COME BEFORE THE LAW?

None of this should come as any surprise, but there is one fact that deserves attention. "In Defense of Religious America," the essay from which Terry Eastland's quotes have been taken, was printed in the June 1981 issue of *Commentary*, the official voice of the American Jewish Committee, an authoritative representative of Jewish opinion in America. The reader will search in vain throughout that issue for a note of introduction, comment, or any kind of critical perspective. This might be less disturbing if each of Eastland's points, beginning with his insistence upon "Christian" values that predate the law, had not served so frequently in the past as a historical basis for racial discrimination. While this does not mean that those events are about to repeat themselves, they are nevertheless evoked by Terry Eastland's morally passionate but logically and historically disputable article. Naturally, there is an explanation for something which strict critical evaluation would show to be ambiguous and unconvincing.

In the first place, both sides of the alliance between non-

Christian conservative groups and the neo-Christian coalition seem to consider their union more than just a marriage of convenience. Second, the antiliberal hostility of the new Christian and new conservatives transcends religious affiliation. In other words, the recent turn of religious events in America has created a strong polarization into liberal and conservative camps, and this polarization could easily become an obsession. Third, the members of the new coalition have voiced their hostility in attempts to "impose" rather than persuade. What is more, this pattern extends to even those groups that ought to be historically wary of impositions as expressed through legislation devised in the name of religious principles. Last, this new state of affairs has been fueled by a cultural and psychological climate that breeds acceptance of the concept by which God is superior and neutral and thus transcends law and history.

In December 1981, the Op-Ed page of the *New York Times* featured various articles in which Catholic leaders expressed the same appreciation of fundamentalist and conservative evangelicalism as *Commentary* showed in deciding to print Eastland's article. Both these forces seem to have chosen the same line of defense, which was that "anything in favor of God should be approved," as though any mention whatsoever of God could suddenly elevate the speaker to righteousness.

The reader will have observed that the passages quoted in these pages from neo-Christian literature make it very clear that this is not just any God; it is a specific God with an unequivocal historical image and equally unmistakable political affiliations. If this partisan and politicized God, so perfectly molded to the needs of a particular group, has managed to overcome the resistance of many and gain the reverence of large opinion groups, the implication must be that a prevalent "desire for God" does actually exist in modern American culture. On the other hand, this desire is currently being exploited to serve a clearly ideological cause. The size and duration of this misuse might go unnoticed if not for the "proof" of religious belief that neo-Christians seem to require of even nonbelievers. It is from this viewpoint that the entire situation should be analyzed.

THE ORIGINS OF TODAY'S DESIRE FOR RELIGION

The desire for God has led to an upsurge of participation in religious demonstrations, as well as increased attempts to promote the religious experience to individually and socially central status. Certainly this has been the most visible and characteristic feature of the seventies and eighties in America. And it does not seem hazardous to guess that it will continue to dominate American society, behavior, and culture through the rest of this century, just as it seems likely that this overall religious cause will continue to shatter periodically into different and even conflicting episodes. Of course it is true that the inner need for spirituality and morality might eventually widen the American outlook on reality, world relations, and the events of life. But it is also true that this inner need may produce tensions and rituals that could easily convert to intolerance and eventually isolate the country from its present busy exchange of ideas and culture with the rest of the world.

The first thing that must be acknowledged is the scope of the trend. Next, each of its countless sources should be examined, even if the result may only be comprehension of the external, sociological aspect. Clearly, the inner personal need for God cannot be explained by social discussion, but significant indications can be seen in the ways this need materializes.

1. *The return to different religious identities may be one result of rediscovering one's ethnic identity.* In 1965, Nathan Glazer and Daniel Patrick Moynihan shot to fame when they wrote *Beyond the Melting Pot.* In their book, the two sociologists claimed the idea of original identities dissolving and then blending to form a common "American identity" was becoming a thing of the past. They went on to hypothesize that in a prosperous postindustrial society it would no longer be helpful to use cultural identities as an indication of America's social composition.

But during the past two decades, the country's distinct ethnic backgrounds have once again come into focus. This is not to say that the fabric of America has frayed, nor that the commonly shared character traits have disappeared. Nevertheless, it has become clear that other original traits have not only not perished but have in fact continued to thrive and are destined to coexist in harmony with the common American identity. More the discovery of a latent reality than the creation of a new factor, this unexpected situation was touched off by the intense efforts of blacks to gain the civil rights they had previously been denied. At first, the movement called for the right to blend into the national identity. But as conflict raged around this initial demand, unforeseen polarizations began to form. In the end, the civil rights movement gave birth to a strong sense of black identity. At the same time, partly in contrast and partly as a response to other tensions, the Jewish and Italian-American communities began to reinforce their own ethnic identities.

More recent arrivals such as the Puerto Ricans, Caribbeans, Mexicans, and Greeks never even started the assimilation process to which the previous immigrants had been submitted, a process it was thought would eventually create a melting pot. They came to America with their own distinct identities, and they have kept and even strengthened those identities. Some of these groups, particularly the Mexicans and Cubans, have exalted their ethnic differences to such an extent that the general public has felt threatened by mass invasion. This situation has led to the discussion of one previously unthinkable legal solution, which was to create a guest worker category in America. While it resembles the provision that already existed in Europe, this expedient will be defintely something new in the heart of a country and a culture that have always been intolerant of anything but the "American" identity.

Religion has been one immediate expression of this group reorganization. It has become harder and harder for Italian-Americans to avoid identification with the Catholic Church, even though disciplined worship and homogeneous belief was never considered typical of Italian immigrants before. American Jews are now almost automatically identified with their faith, if not with its worship. And the way black religion has voiced demands, constituted social organization, and inspired unified strength is well known throughout America. In reflection, other religious groups have felt the need to reorganize and reinforce their own identities, even when there is no ethnic "necessity" or cultural diversity to declare or defend. The entire country has been affected by this new phase, in which responses have become more exorbitant as the questions have become more urgent. This search for new religious expressions has been accelerated by at least two other factors: on the one hand, the "otherness" of ethnic identity, once considered a handicap, was now celebrated as a privilege. On the other hand, the problems of postindustrial society and world conditions gave rise to increasingly complicated demands and the need for urgent solutions to be found on solid, indisputable ground.

2. *Religious belief can be a buffer for the world's complications.* After the sixties, with their secular and political overthrow of faith, the masses in America and the rest of the advanced industrialized world began to consider the complex problems of the world as little more than irritating complications. But these "complications" have led to bitter dispute even among the leading experts, and they have caused continually forming and reforming polarizations. A system which once seemed airtight has now sprung a series of leaks that ooze with anxiety and instability. People are trapped in an unbearable sense of inadequacy to deal with those problems. Mostly, this inadequacy is blamed on technology, as people who ought to possess the means and experience to solve the problems flounder; and on culture, inasmuch as no tranquilizing explanations can be offered. When things are so hopeless, the impulse to retreat to the realm of religion is inevitable. Still, it would be unfair to say that religion has only been an easy way out or the response of the simpleminded. It is reasonable and human to turn to religion as compensation for frustration with the complexity and enormity of problems. The desire to retreat to a less precarious territory is understandable. This type of escape also implies that the feelings of inadequacy and impotence have been attributed

to a secular society forsaken by God's light, and it is only natural to want to abandon such a society in search of new guidance.

This may explain the charismatic nature inherent in neo-Christianity, with its emphasis on such dramatic aspects as pentecostalism, the Jesus experience, and the on-the-spot personal conversion that changes one's life. The dissemination of these untraditional and anticultural ways of diving headfirst into the religious experience belies a sense of panic and urgency that will not brook gradual transition. Similarly, there is no room here for thoughtful mediation between secular and religious worlds or between withdrawn spiritual life and extroverted social organization, the master achievement of the mainstream churches. The new converts, sects, and cults shroud themselves in salvation, and their only communication is the cry for mass exodus. Their strongly anticultural appeals bespeak a deep-felt mistrust of scholarship and intellectual solutions; eventually this mistrust turns into antagonism. According to this perspective, the way out can be neither cultural nor intellectual, because the prevailing culture itself is the source of all the complications, evils, and risks from which the masses are fleeing.

Yet, there is one more way to respond. Here, the negative tones are reinforced by surefire assertions; there are no feelings of inferiority with respect to culture, the proposals of which are not even indirectly acknowledged. Of course this attitude is not new, but in its present form it is more drastic than ever before. In this outlook, religion becomes science, or a universal and totalitarian system of interpretation and leadership. At least two of America's traditional Protestant churches and cults, the Christian Science Church and the Jehovah's Witnesses, have envisioned religion as a kind of science. Both these sects see the scientific nature of faith as the surest and most direct route to salvation. Because He is the source, Jesus is *also* science, and no theory or technique can ever be truer. In actual fact, this position has been and still is expressed more as a rejection of scientific solutions (witness the refusal of medicine) than as

an alternate solution to the problems of life. Now many fundamentalist churches tend to equate religion with science, forbid
medical intervention, and preach faith healing.

It is at this point that the religious movement called Scientology comes in, with a certain degree of success. The jargon
and rituals of Scientology have been designed to create a sense
of modernity, technical update, and progress toward the future, all of which give it the aura of science fiction literature.
And it is no coincidence that the movement's founder and chief
minister, Ron Hubbard, was a prolific author of science fiction
stories before he turned to theology. In *Religious and Spiritual
Groups in America* (1973), Robert Ellwood, a professor of the
history of religion at the University of Southern California, has
analyzed Hubbard's religious texts of the past ten years and
compared them to the same man's science fiction writing of the
forties. Ellwood believes he can show parallel themes linking
the future world imagined by the writer to the church founded
three decades later by the preacher. The basic idea is of a trap,
in which reality is a prisoner of fantasy. Of course, fantasy is a
child of the mind, and the mind can undergo alterations or dis-
turbances that do not come from within but originate in the
"environment," just as a spaceship can be sucked into a black
hole or a plane can disappear over the Bermuda triangle.

The Scientology Church expresses its theology in words and
concepts that do indeed evoke a spaceship, whose crew shares
the risks, camaraderie, and exaltations of victory. The spaceship serves as a continual reminder of the danger all around us.
It is no great task to cook up an answer for fear when that fear
comes from lost faith in science and technology, alienation from
prevailing culture, and mistrust in the control exercised by universities and research centers. But Scientology embellishes this
response with instruments, machines, and measurements that
play the same role as the sacraments or rituals in other churches.

As so often happens, it is hard to pinpoint the success of
Scientology statistically, because little reliable data is available.
The cult has been loudly attacked by other churches and the

scientific establishment, all of which claim Hubbard's proposals
are a colossal fraud. But the issue is not so much to evaluate
the situation as to identify the symptoms it indicates. The insecurity and hopelessness that can produce this type of cult and
its success are clear. Obviously, Scientology diverges from the
charismatic, Pentacostal, and neo-Christian sects, because it seeks
its answer to complication not in simplification but in areas that
stray widely from those of traditional culture and politics.
Moreover, it replaces traditional science with faith in "another"
science, whose guarantee lies in a mixture of psychological
training methods and inner illuminations the premises of which
are thus "received" rather than verified by common knowledge.

3. *Religion as identity for emerging new groups.* Opinion polls
and religious literature in America often repeat one vital statis-
tic, which is that most followers of the new cults are young
people. But these are no longer the wild and reckless teens of
the sixties. In this context, "young people" means adults with
a realistic and practical outlook on life, whether that outlook has
been acquired at a university or in the workplace. The mention
of universities here may seen to contradict the heavy anti-intellectualism and anticultural hostility repeatedly mentioned in
descriptions of these new sects. But most of today's students
experience the university as a practical training course in which
mass education is used to prepare them for concrete career activities. Faculties of religion almost never serve as breeding
grounds for these new cults. On the contrary, these departments are most often seen as repositories of establishment culture, and as such must be studiously avoided. And indeed, these
faculties are often seen as the hotbeds of the "secular humanism" the fundamentalists detest. So the new cults recruit their
followers elsewhere, most frequently from schools of engineer-
ing, economics, business administration, political science. The
people they enroll have usually acquired some control over small
territories, but they are most likely anxious about their inability to control the large areas where those threatening and ir-
resoluble problems are formed.

Another aspect that always seems to emerge from research on the new religions is that most neo-Christians come from the middle-class white population. This does not mean that America's new religions are irrevocably white, middle-class, and educated. It may be that this highly mobile group, with its many privileges and opportunities for success, has more reason to fear the unknown and events it cannot control. Furthermore, this group's identity is bland and innocuous, hard to affirm, and even harder to defend. New churches and religious movements can help to raise this identity threshold by creating strong, clear-cut bonds and consolidating an image as visible and recognizable as other ethnic identities, so that the group can compete successfully. This is where the roots of conservatism and neo-Christianity lie, and it is the source of the alliance between new religion and the aggressive activism of the new conservatives.

It would be wrong to think that this impulse to identify the group and its interests is the only motivation behind the seemingly widespread phenomenon of these new religions. The reasons must run wider and deeper. And yet without this psychological, sociological, and historical frame of reference, it would be hard to interpret what looks like a contradiction in terms. On the one hand, there is celebration of a superior, neutral God. On the other, there is a tendency to use God in direct defense of the interests and viewpoints of particular groups.

Of course there are those who sincerely believe that their own political views are the secular fulfillment of a neutral God's will and as such are nonnegotiable. But there are signs that the many new religions in America are choosing sides on God's battlefield. We have seen that Protestantism has been divided into two factions: the mainstream churches that defend "liberal" positions, and the new conservative sects. The Catholic Church has likewise polarized into two segments of opinion, one involved almost exclusively in opposing abortion, the other preoccupied with social problems; these diverse branches have separated despite the common theology they share. The same holds true for Jewish culture, which is polarizing around the old liberal views and the new conservatism. So it becomes apparent that the idea of a neutral God can be undermined by serious political division. This was proved in late 1980 by the furor that surrounded Argentina's persecution of Jacobo Timerman. Another example has been the violent neo-Christian campaign against "secular humanism." Because both episodes have the same political overtones (despite their completely different protagonists) and because they have involved millions of believers, they are pertinent to our discussion.

TIMERMAN AND AMERICAN JEWISH OPINION

For years, Jacobo Timerman was a leading exponent of the Zionist movement in Argentina, where he was managing editor of the prestigious newspaper *La Opinion*. As he describes it in *Prisoner Without a Name, Cell Without a Number*, for more than two years Timerman was a political prisoner of the Argentine regime, allegedly because of his paper's progressive stance. Timerman's masterful ability to describe his ordeal of torture and absolute seclusion might be the only thing setting him apart from thousands of other Argentine prisoners if not for the fact that his jailers never mentioned his political positions, in all the thirty months of his incarceration. The only accusation he ever faced was that he was "a Zionist and a Jew." In the spring of 1981, Timerman testified before the Foreign Affairs Commission of the United States Senate, to show that the persecution of Jews accused of Zionism and involvement in evil international conspiracy had not ended with the defeat of the Nazi regime but was still very much a living practice. Evidence gathered by the State Department and the Senate supported Timerman's testimony, and so the American Jewish community immediately rallied around the cause. What could be more natural for a culture which had consolidated its identity in the concentration camps of the Holocaust?

Then suddenly the issue—a moral, religious, and human one—took on a political cast, and in so doing alienated part of America's Jews from Jacobo Timerman. How could such a culturally and historically unnatural situation have occurred? A New York newspaper, *Jewish Week & American Examiner,* printed numerous articles signed by Jewish leaders, including Richard Yaffe's full-page piece, which appeared on June 7, 1981, under the title, "Timerman: Martyr or Opportunist? Idolized as a Hero and Despised as an Adventurer." These attacks were supported by Irving Kristol, whose *Wall Street Journal* column hinted that Timerman might have dangerous links with international terrorism. William Safire was more prudent, but he was no less doubtful about Timerman's personal morality. William Buckley, Jr., the conservative Catholic writer, claimed he had had confirmation of Timerman's shady political affiliations and moral ambivalence from the mouth of Simon Wiesenthal, director of the Documentation Center in Vienna. Some Jewish leaders seemed to have struck an accord with non-Jews conservative in their attempts to isolate a fellow Jewish personality who claimed to have been persecuted for his religion and not his political militancy. The first person to stand in Timerman's defense was Simon Wiesenthal, who quickly denied that he had ever stated any opinion regarding the Argentine newsman and added that he believed Timerman's allegations of anti-Semitism. On June 27, 1981, the *New York Times* produced evidence of "special" treatment supposedly reserved for Jewish political prisoners in Argentina, and finally, Robert Weisbrot published a dramatic article in the same week's *New Republic,* offering wide support for the thesis that the flame of anti-Semitism had been rekindled in a pro-Western country whose regime had firm links to the United States.

The American segment of Timerman's destiny was unsettling and unprecedented, and it showed that the neutral God of the renewed Judeo-Christian alliance can be forced to protect one political side, representing not all Jews but some Jews chosen on the basis not of religion but of political affiliation. Timerman is now back in Argentina, after the return of democracy to that country. But he lived in exile, in Israel, a highly unlikely venue for "a left-wing terrorist." Never since his release from prison has he ceased to identify himself with his cultural and religious background. His political "deviation" may seem serious in the eyes of a military junta, but it is certainly within the limits of free democratic debate.

Should we thus conclude that the direction approved by the official political wings of neo-Christianity and politically conservative Jewish groups is a narrow path that demands strict discipline and a continuous risk of contamination? One sure thing is that it does require a declaration of political preference, and this is a novelty in post-Holocaust Judaism. It would seem to indicate that the Christian part of the conservative Judeo-Christian coalition has been able to bring its political choices to bear upon the solidarity that always existed between the Jewish community and one persecuted Jew.

This argument could be supported by the example of those four Catholic nuns, most likely "liberals," who were shot by Salvadoran soldiers: the conservative Christian coalition was no more merciful to them than it was to Timerman. But it must be kept in mind that the nuns were not killed because of their religion, nor were they ever persecuted for this reason. Theirs were merely four more deaths in a war between the anti- and progovernment factions of a tiny Latin American republic. On the other hand, Timerman seems to have been persecuted precisely because he represented something intolerable in another Latin American drama, inasmuch as he was an outspoken Jewish leader. And yet he was actively isolated in the United States by many of those very Jewish leaders who should have defended him. On the other hand, the part of Jewish culture that feels uncomfortable with the new Christians and their crusades and is suspicious of a religious fervor that can so easily become political or discriminatory found the Timerman affair a cause for serious concern.

THE CRUSADE AGAINST "SECULAR HUMANISM"

Others have watched in shock as neo-Christianity has acquired political militancy in the America of the eighties, and they have been worried, frequently alarmed by some of its episodes. The most important of these incidents is what the press has dubbed "the war against secular humanism." In Congress the front has been led by Senator Jesse Helms, a celebrated champion of neo-Christianity. Generally speaking, secular humanism stands for any value judgment that appears to differ from Christian doctrine. As Helms says, "In essence we must raise faith in God against the values of secular humanism."

It is a little more difficult to decide exactly what secular humanism is. The answer seems to be, "Any interpretation of events that is not mentioned in the Scriptures." But that the issue is considerably more complicated was brought home in a letter to the editor of a Plano, Texas, newspaper. Sara Pyle's June 10, 1981, letter gained notoriety as an "antisecular" manifesto after it was widely reprinted throughout the Christian press and later picked up by the *New York Times*.

Plano's neo-Christian citizen railed against the type of exam her children's teachers had been using, and she furiously objected to tests that require students to give their own value judgments. She considered dangerous and misleading such questions as, "Which freedom would you save if you could have only one: political, economic, or religious?" and "Which of these two possibilities frightens you most: being forced to marry a girl because she is pregnant or having to marry a person of another race?"

Announcing that she had rescued her own children from the influence of public schools, Pyle went on to say she opposed sex education because its very existence indicated "a tendency to indoctrinate young people." As for the origins of life, Pyle rejected both Darwin and the right of teachers to mention his theory. Being herself a person of no little erudition, she reminded her readers that "all this" ("this" being America's modern mass education system) was born "under the leadership of John Dewey, father of progressive education." The reference to Dewey and his acknowledged title seemed to her to be sufficient reason for indignation, inasmuch as the author did not bother to elaborate on that specific condemnation.

Because the ties linking Sara Pyle to Senator Helms, this must be evaluated as one of the ways that America's new religious spirit tends to express itself. On the one hand, there is the "Plano manifesto," with its formula that "religious rigor must not bend to the needs of politics and political life. Let them bend to it." On the other there is the Timerman case, in which the formula seems to be upended. "Timerman may be a good Jew and Zionist, but he is suspected of harboring political preferences that cannot be forgiven."

These two facets of fundamentalism seem to exist side by side. The only way to interpret them is to consider the rise of Christian fundamentalism within a frame of reference not unlike that which corresponds to religious and political fundamentalism in the Islamic world and to the no less passionate and intransigent fervor of some members of the Gush Emunin movement in Israel. The swing to fundamentalism implies both an affirmation and a negation. The affirmation says that God's neutrality keeps him completely untainted by day-to-day controversy. The negation states that this controversy has already been resolved and so therefore nothing is negotiable or subject to value judgments. "God has already decided," chant the doomsayers. But the game plan for those controversies has yet to be drawn up, and so someone must be elected to do it. The only competent authority seems to be religious leadership, and thus there is danger that this situation will lead to an antidemocratic or at least highly biased imposition of views, tantamount to spiritual conversion. America's new religious belief is certainly not limited to the conflictual territory of hard-core fundamentalism. But neo-Christianity's exalted tones, aggressive style, political rigor, and unwillingness to adapt create a blinding light that attracts a great deal of attention to the phenomenon of faith while distorting or altogether impeding level-headed comprehension of the many ways in which this new demand for religion is being expressed in America.

IN SEARCH OF NEW VALUES

Religious fervor seems to inspire behavior patterns typical of emerging social groups. But as we have seen, this particular religious belief is not related to the arrival of new groups on the social stage. What is new here are the setting and social conditions. In this sense, "new" means "different." The world and its society have changed, and what most people know about these changes is not reassuring. Such physical values as money, property, and objects are no longer guaranteed; there is no legislative continuity in a world where people who think they have certain rights are suddenly stripped of them; social assurance falters when groups are suspect and in fact do betray one's trust, for whatever reason; there is no racial peace when every ethnic group feels threatened and mutual hostility raises the threshold of defense.

Today's world calls out for safe refuge and sure compensation. Thus the emerging group that has turned to religion as a last-chance shelter can no longer be socially circumscribed and historically traced with the same ease that existed for earlier groups. What is happening is a sort of invisible migration, in which each person tries to relocate life's equilibrium, removing it from elusive reality and storing it in a safe imaginary world. It may be painful to watch this movement from life to a dream, or from reality—be it beautiful or ugly—to pure and simple hope. But this has occurred again and again throughout history.

Even if such absolute security does come hand in hand with minimal theology and a visualization of reality that is as rigorous as it is unfounded, it is only natural that most anxious people will consider it the best place for exile. But as they set off on this sort of pilgrimage, the new Christians are implicitly and unconsciously affirming that "salvation has already come," and thus good and evil (which they call "right" and "wrong") have already been defined once and for all. It is easy to convert the masses to something that has already been discovered and resolved, because there is no way to dispute it. But how does one invest in the hope of future salvation? Whether this desired salvation is Christian or Jewish, it can be wiped out by belief in immediate salvation, and once that belief has been accepted, it transforms history into stone, replacing the past with the future and erecting thick walls against any threat of change. Within this secure citadel, the lines of judgment have already been drawn, once and forever.

SIGNS OF APOCALYPSE AND THE ROADS TO SALVATION

The neo-Christians must constantly show that they have achieved their project for salvation, just as they must prove that any deviation from it (the sin they call "secular humanism") is a form of intolerable arrogance. They seem to derive their stamina from the apocalyptic interpretation of everything they see. To them, the world is a flurry of disturbingly ambiguous relations between the periphery and its core, the people and their leaders, the base and its summit. They listen in anguish to the concurring and contrasting opinions of equally illustrious experts, and in the end they reject them all. Besieged as they are by needs, doubts, and such incomprehensible realities as cultural and racial barriers, they try to escape isolation by establishing iron-clad bonds. But if these bonds are to hold in the face of steadily shifting reality, unreliable history, and faceless politics, they must be secured not in expectations of future salvation but in a guarantee of salvation that has already been achieved. This is the only way to establish such a determined commitment to hold firm, be it on cultural, political, or social fronts. And it explains the conservative passions of masses who have little to conserve, in real terms.

America's call for religion has developed alongside an arid, technical, spiritless culture known as survivalism, by which limited groups of disciples adopt and practice techniques that will allow them to survive the destruction all others will be unable to escape. Becoming survivalists means that the neo-Christians must accept that culture's discipline and intolerance. One typical feature shared by survivalism and neo-Christianity is the denial of future opportunity for salvation to others. Only those who accept salvation now, when danger is barely visible, and only those who have rigorously conformed to behavior patterns that might be called "preventive" will earn the right to a second chance. In other words, the faith bloc that has resulted from the convergence of political conservatism, neo-Christianity, and survivalism refuses to see farther than the lines that have already been drawn. This leaves mainstream Christianity wondering whether its most recent offshoot has not already broken through the lines of Christian culture, by pushing up the moment of judgment and salvation to an arbitrary "now" chosen by the survivalists and unconfirmed in the Scriptures.

Nor have many black churches escaped this compulsion to erect rigid barriers and set down indisputable truths. This may cause violent conflict some day, if intransigence can erode the open ecumenism of such preaching as Martin Luther King's, dedicated to building bridges of understanding with "the other side," to overcome the opposition that generated the conflict between "friends and enemies," "brothers and oppressors."

Yet another aspect of the problem and its origins harks back to an important thesis developed by Italian sociologist Francesco Alberoni. Technology, industrial society, the development of medicine, psychology, the social sciences, the availability of an arsenal of electronic gadgets, have all accustomed the postindustrial generation to the reassuring value of universal control. Today everything can be controlled—or so was the general persuasion until a few years ago—from fevers to gold, the stock market, weapons, orbiting missiles, occasional unruly storms, the inside of cells, plant diseases, the transmission of genes, a person's moods, and even the length of his life. This has been the impression left in the wake of all the glorification of technology and science. But now this control seems to be slipping. Terrorists rampage; stock markets race out of control; monetary values skyrocket, to the complete surprise of the experts; the price of gold dips and soars; jobs lose their values; and personal identity, even life itself, become meaningless.

Naturally, the consequences are suspicion, then mistrust, and finally outright rejection of the instruments of that control, products of a self-assured secular society that even extended the techniques of control to social problems. Once, that society made it possible to reduce suffering and intergroup friction, lower the threshold of suspicion and division, wipe out conflict, and thus improve life. The apparatus which devised such thorough control of social mechanisms was called "liberalism"; it was part of the industrial society, despite its occasional apparent opposition to that society. In a June 2, 1981 *Wall Street Journal* article, Arthur Schlesinger, Jr., warned the financial community of America that it was dangerous to reject liberalism. He said that by showing it was possible to achieve a better world without revolution or upheaval, liberalism had actually protected industrial civilization.

Schlesinger offered a powerful argument. Yet the alienation of America's "silent majority" was more than just a shrug of the shoulders; it was a deeply felt and widespread mistrust in society's control techniques, and it sent people running for cover. Politically, one response was conservatism, imagined as a sort of magic "universal freeze." But the understandable yearning for certainty conflicts with man's inability to halt the progression of history, with its continual production of unforeseeable events that will not conform to the rules of the past.

Religion, or at least the renewed fervor of the new Christians, responds to every future possibility by withdrawing one more delegation of authority. Its members want passionately to believe that the world has exhausted all its reserve programs for secular salvation. America's new coalition of political and religious forces constitutes an important bloc that will not easily be overcome. But as Schlesinger pointed out, denying history and limiting options for the future are the most anti-industrial, anticapitalist gestures that can ever be made.

The reader may wonder why so much significance has been assigned to the funamentalist and conservative part of American Christianity. After all, there is a chance that this new religious impulse will conclude in a sensible equilibrium with other

visions and religious needs. But several questions remain un-
answered, and it is these responses, not some simple state of
equilibrium based on good common sense, that will determine
whether the future of religious and social life in America will
be serene or conflictual.

One problem is that the observer of religion as a political
phenomenon can say very little indeed about the purely internal exigence called faith. If the fears and worries we have mentioned really do prevail, if this new faith is truly and only a safe
refuge, then it will become an intransigent catalyst of conflict
and the perfect exasperation of political ideas. But if the inner
nature of relations between the individual and God prevails, then
religious belief will dissolve conflict rather than stimulate it.

I have said that any examination of the neo-Christian religions must also account for the fervor of such differently inspired religious movements as the ones based on meditation,
which withdraw from reality not in search of safe refuge but to
relate to it differently. But there is little information about the
size and strength of these movements It is doubtful whether
this type of belief, as alien as it is to industrial society and its
needs, can compensate for the political militancy of the New
Christian Right. Still, there is a chance that it will encourage a
return to cooperation based upon new ideas drawn from both
history and from man's endless imagination.

As for liberal Christianity, socially committed Catholicism, and
the large part of the Jewish faith and culture which knows that
most of its adventure still lies ahead, everything will depend
upon how realistically each of these groups can measure the
challenge of fundamentalist and evangelical religions. Equally
significant are the relations these religions will maintain or re-
establish with industrial society, so often dismissed as an enemy and thus abandoned to the "protection" of conservative
Christianity. And here lies a rarely mentioned but obvious contradiction. Fundamentalism and evangelicalism seem to be great
supporters of capitalist development, or at least they seem to
want to give this impression. But they are also the cause of di

vision and conflict, whereas industrial society only prospers where harmony prevails; they emphasize a type of salvation that has already been established, whereas industrial society must always march onward; they demand rigid, nonnegotiable behavior, whereas the very nature of industrial society makes it inclined to pragmatism and compromise; they require constant demonstration that no change has taken place, whereas industrial society is the very embodiment of change, extending even to values and customs; and they are deeply mistrustful of mechanisms that serve to balance different impulses and needs, whereas these mechanisms are the most genuine invention of the industrial society.

When survivalism becomes the rule of conduct, room for development shrinks and demand for spiritual values shrivels. But the likelihood that this will ever occur depends upon whether the conditions of crisis and emergency (or the impression that such conditions exist) are dissolved by future political moves, by the reestablishment of economic equilibrium where uncertainty prevails, or by the abating of international tensions. Doomsday anxiety and the search for absolute responses stem mostly from fear. As America's second century of industrial life draws to an end, the nation's social behavior and religious choices will be determined by that fear and whether it lingers, snowballs, or disappears altogether.